120 Ways
To
Achieve
Your
Purpose
With
LinkedIn™

Tried and True

Tips and Techniques

Sue Ellson

Published by

❧ 120 Ways Publishing PO Box 65, Surrey Hills, Victoria, Australia, 3127
120ways@120ways.com Book: B0002

Printed by

IngramSpark, Unit A1/A3, 7 Janine Street, Scoresby, Victoria, Australia 3179
ingramsparkinternational@ingramcontent.com

National Library of Australia Cataloguing-in-Publication entry

Ellson, Sue, 1965 – Author
120 Ways to Achieve Your Purpose With LinkedIn™
Tried And True Tips And Techniques / Sue Ellson
ISBN-10: 0-9942875-0-X ISBN 13: 978-0-9942875-0-2 (paperback)
Includes index. Books – Business, Books – Internet

DEDICATION

For my children,
Carmen and Peter,
whom I love more
than words can say.

ACKNOWLEDGEMENTS

Enduring thanks over many years for the constant love, support and faith in my abilities to Bernie and Wendy Ellson, Lee Llewellyn AM, Grace Guo, Cathie Lording, Melinda Hume-Cook, Jacquie Wise and Ângelo Klin.

Special thanks more recently to Suzanne Dunlop for our extremely productive Accountability Partnership and Colin Freckleton for our Summer Series Program.

Thanks and kudos to all of my past clients, students, friends and family for inspiring me to gather all of these insights in one location.

Thanks to Euan Mitchell for his author consulting services, Avanska Design for the book cover concept, Colleen Bate and Vaughne Geary for proof reading the content and Aaron Brendel for his website development assistance.

Thanks to you, the reader, for investing in yourself.

I now encourage you to read on and start getting excited about choosing the various ways you will be able to achieve your purpose with LinkedIn.

You can stay fully updated in relation to this book and the other 120 Ways Publishing publications by joining the 120 Ways Publishing Membership Program at http://120ways.com/members

Contents

Preface

'120 Ways To Achieve Your Purpose With LinkedIn: Tried And True Tips And Techniques' is for:

- defining and achieving your purpose

- managing your LinkedIn Profile, Company Page and Group

- exploring LinkedIn features including Newsfeed, Pulse, Apps

- job search, career development, business and social enterprise

- measuring and improving your performance, statistics, backups

- solving issues, taking action and achieving results

It includes information for:

- students, job seekers and career changers

- freelancers, entrepreneurs and business owners

- advisers, consultants and thought leaders

- community groups and professional associations

- schools, colleges and universities

- anyone who wants to leverage their skills, knowledge and networks

This thorough, practical and detailed guide provides you with the key strategies and techniques, based on your purpose, that you can implement today for your success in the future.

Get started and take action now!

**Special free bonus offers at http://120ways.com/members

Introduction

Are you clear about your purpose in life?

If the answer is yes, well done!

If the answer is no, don't worry, it will come!

Do you already know a lot about LinkedIn?

If the answer is yes, fantastic, you are about to learn a lot more!

If the answer is no, I am so happy that you are willing to learn!

'120 Ways To Achieve Your Purpose With LinkedIn' has been written to help you choose what aspects of LinkedIn will be useful for your job or enterprise purpose - and give you the courage to complete the right steps to achieve results.

So get ready to take action!

TAKE ACTION

Action beats hesitation

Doing beats hoping

Persistence beats defeat

Opportunity beats regret

Starting beats stalling

Motivation beats limitation

Courage beats comfort

Striving beats stalling

Leading beats following

Knowing beats doubting

Choice beats limitation

Answers beat assumptions

Now beats never

Take action

Quotes from 2016 radio advertisements
for Victoria University http://vu.edu.au

Hello there! My name is Sue Ellson and I am an Independent LinkedIn Specialist. I am not paid or endorsed by LinkedIn – but I am here to help you achieve your purpose with LinkedIn.

This book includes a range of tried and true tips and techniques based on successful results from personal experience, consulting, training, writing, broadcasting and research in a variety of different areas – job search, recruitment, human resources, business, marketing, branding, social media, information technology, search engine optimization and more!

I joined LinkedIn on 21 December 2003 and am one of the first 100,000 members in the world – in fact, I am number 77,832 – and you can verify this fact by visiting http://linkedin.com/profile/view?id=77832.

I have personally overcome the challenges of downsizing, retrenchment, dismissal, delayed contract starts, cancelled contracts, irregular income, late payments from clients, unsuccessful interviews, illegal employer practices and lengthy periods where I could not secure paid work due to other personal circumstances.

Several of these situations have occurred multiple times throughout my life. I have also had direct exposure to the issues of disability, racism, discrimination, long term unemployment and underemployment.

As a result of these experiences, I sincerely hope that if you are currently in any one of these situations yourself, you believe that there is still hope and opportunity available – because I certainly do!

I really want to help you achieve your purpose – just like I have helped so many of my clients from around the world!

I also do not believe that any situation is ever completely hopeless. It simply means that you will need to be a little more creative when you choose your solutions (and that may involve going through a number of stages to reach a successful outcome).

I like helping people identify their strengths. For the most part, I ignore any weaknesses because I believe our strengths are there to help us achieve our purpose.

I have worked with secondary school students, unskilled workers, technical experts, academics, professionals, consultants, business owners, enterprises (for profit and not for profit), senior executives, portfolio career workers, semi-retirees, retirees, corporate advisers and more.

I have also worked with a lot of very successful individuals, small enterprises, large corporations and associations and have provided them with practical advice that has generated both short term and long term results. This has been very beneficial financially, and that income has enabled me to spend a lot of my time on various not for profit and advocacy initiatives.

But let's get back to you! This book has been designed to be useful for a range of people with a range of purposes. Whilst LinkedIn is promoted as a network for professionals, it is one of the most highly optimized social media platforms for Google Search Results.

For example, when someone completes a search with your name, keywords or enterprise name, there is a very good chance that your LinkedIn Profile will appear (if you have included your keywords in your content). This is very important because when someone does a search on Google, 75% of the click-throughs are likely to go to one of the top three search results.

My most successful clients usually see me more than once. The most common sequence is that we meet for two hours and I teach them what to do with LinkedIn for their purpose and then they complete a range of homework on their own with a variety of templates and guides (this can take up to 10 hours).

We re-convene and go over that information and maximize it for their purpose (one or two sessions of two hours). Then they start implementing their strategies and tactics on their own and we re-convene to review their performance (two hours).

We then schedule six monthly one hour review sessions and I provide details of the latest changes to LinkedIn and we tweak their content and strategy once again.

Some of my clients find it difficult to complete all of the written information needed for a LinkedIn Profile. They usually tell me that they can write for other people but not for themselves.

I think most people, when they are not distracted, like listening to good stories. In fact, the better your story is on LinkedIn – the better your results! If you can incorporate your key values, just imagine how much closer you will be to your purpose!

So, for clients who struggle with the writing process, I work with them to help them produce the written content and we have had some incredible results. This is more expensive up front in terms of hours of consulting service, but it usually delivers much faster results. For people who find it difficult to write, it can actually save them many hours of time and frustration!

The famous author Stephen King was asked, "How do you write?" He says, "One word at a time." Not surprisingly, his answer is usually dismissed. So he qualifies his answer and says, "But that is all it is. It sounds too simple to be true, but consider the Great Wall of China, if you will: one stone at a time, man. That's all. One stone at a time. But I've read you can see that **** from space without a telescope."

Ironically in a conversation, a lot of people like talking about themselves! So if you get stuck writing about yourself or your enterprise, just imagine you are talking to someone else rather than writing to someone else.

You may also like to incorporate some images on your LinkedIn Profile so that you can tell part of your story in a visual way. Did you know that the human brain can process images 600 times faster than text? But just remember that computer programs still rely on words for searches.

You will see that I mention asking for help several times throughout this book. I am only one person in one time zone of the world, so I am not expecting to be able to personally help every person who reads this book (although I really love working with individuals and training enterprise teams).

If you find it difficult to complete any of the suggestions in this book, please consider sourcing some extra personal assistance so that you can achieve your purpose as soon as possible.

You may also like to consider working in partnership with a trusted friend, accountability partner, colleague or mentor so that you can both motivate each other (although I do recommend that you only do it for a maximum of two hours at a time or take very regular breaks because it can be emotionally challenging to go through all of these suggestions and compile so much historical information all at once).

I would also like to encourage you to join our 120 Ways Publishing Membership Program at http://120ways.com/members as the Premium offering includes access to Instructional Videos and Audio Recordings.

If you can't find something you are looking for in this book please:

- see if it is listed in the Index

- join the 120 Ways Publishing Membership Program at http://120ways.com/members

- visit the LinkedIn Help Center at http://help.linkedin.com/app/home/

- contact me directly via http://sueellson.com (where you will also find a huge range of free publications and presentations that will also help you realize your potential)

- source a local professional through a local career development association (some of these are listed in Appendix 1)

- contact a coaching or counselling professional with expertise in these areas.

Jobs and Enterprises

I have used the descriptions of 'jobs' and 'enterprises' throughout this book. Jobs is related to finding employment, paid or unpaid, within an enterprise.

Enterprises could be a business, organization, multi-national company, association, educational institution, government body, advocacy group or collective etc that is either large or small, for profit or not for profit.

You will observe in my writing that I have a very strong moral compass and I am only interested in ethical personal development and enterprise practice.

I trust that you will only use this information for ethical purposes. This book must not be used for any form of exploitation, manipulation, bullying, racism, discrimination, defamation etc.

There are many ways for every person to achieve their dreams and live a purposeful life without regrets – and in my view, it is possible for everyone to win and no-one to lose. That said, you do need to base your choices and actions on solid research, tried and true tips and techniques and respond appropriately to feedback you discover along the way.

You may also be wondering why I believe you can achieve your purpose with LinkedIn (for example – I did not choose Facebook, Twitter, Google+ or some other form of social media).

In my view, LinkedIn has the largest range of potential across the widest range of the population, whether you are a job seeker or an enterprise. It certainly should not be considered as the only part of your success strategy – but I do believe that for most people, it can provide you with a range of ways to help you achieve your job or enterprise purpose.

The major strengths of LinkedIn include:

- longevity (started in 2003)

- adaptability (multiple acquisitions and updates)

- database size (it is one of the most active international social media platforms in terms of individual member participation)

- future focus (constantly innovating)

- revenue streams (multiple sources with new ones added frequently)

- strict user agreement and cyber security protocols

- good quality business practices and employee culture

LinkedIn representatives have told me that LinkedIn wants to make the world's professionals more productive and successful – by building each member's identity, network and knowledge.

Social selling (for either a job or an enterprise), is about a trigger (idea), insights (content) and a referral. To secure a sale, you need to help people make decisions.

This process can also be defined as feed, find and educate. Did you know that up to 75% of sales are based on perceived value and insights?

Although a digital reputation is ultimately based on being omnipresent in a niche – please don't become a nuisance! That will backfire – big time!!

If you would like some more general information and history about LinkedIn, please visit http://press.linkedin.com/about-linkedin

1. It's All About Purpose

If you are going to work on achieving your purpose with LinkedIn you need to choose a purpose first.

Remember that clarity leads to conversion. Confusion leads to chaos.

Most faith or belief systems suggest that you need to define your purpose quite clearly and if you ask authentically, you will receive. I can tell you that it does work. Sometimes it works even better than you expect!

You may have heard of the song by Australian singer and songwriter, Paul Kelly, "Be careful what you pray for – you just might get it." It is one of my favorite tunes – I like the rendition by Vika and Linda Bull!

Action 1: *Remember that clarity leads to conversion – be specific about your purpose and ask appropriately so that you have the opportunity to receive*

1.1 Take Action To Achieve Your Purpose

You might think that a book called '120 Ways To Achieve Your Purpose With LinkedIn' will give you a magical 120 steps and once you complete them – voilà, you will have successfully achieved your purpose!

However, I am quite sure that each person who reads this book is likely to have a slightly different purpose and every suggestion will be open to some form of interpretation (even though I have tried to be as clear as possible).

I am also guessing that most readers will not have the time or inclination to complete 120 tasks to get to where they want to go!

But we all know that to be successful, you must complete the right steps on an ongoing basis and avoid the bad triggers that can take you in the wrong direction. You also need to have the courage to work out how to recover from any steps that don't go so well.

It is also important if you want to shortcut the process to do what works rather than what doesn't work. To choose tried and true tips and techniques rather than the latest fads.

So that is my challenge to you. Don't just read this book, please, TAKE ACTION.

You may be a perfectionist or a procrastinator – and if you are, there is nothing wrong with that – BUT, if you want the best results, you must be courageous and TAKE ACTION. Done is better than perfect!

If this book gives you just one positive action step that you actually complete towards your job or enterprise purpose, I will be happy (after all, I am very easily pleased)!

If you select and complete between one and 20 action steps, I will be very happy (and I would love to hear about it).

Complete 20 or more action steps and I know that YOU will be happy with the results.

This book includes a range of actions you can choose, tasks you can complete and measures you can use to track your performance.

Action 2: *Complete 20 or more action steps from this book and you will be happy*

1.2 Prepare Your Own Action Plan

You may choose to start from the beginning of the book and take action as you go through (feel free to scribble in some notes, use a highlighter pen or bookmark pages) or you might want to skip to a particular section and do what you 'like' or find 'easier' to do first.

You could even read the book and create a 'to-do' action plan list (on paper or in a spreadsheet) as you go along. I don't mind which method you choose as I have tried to make every section a stand-alone piece that you can use on its own.

As the LinkedIn Platform is constantly changing, I have not included screen shots — I will start with a small disclaimer, this information was correct at the time of publication. For this reason, please join the 120 Ways Publishing Membership Program http://120ways.com/members to subscribe to free email updates, free later version update summaries and gain access to the free downloads listed in this book in Section 20.

Whilst the LinkedIn platform will definitely change and adapt in the future, I have tried to include more strategic advice that you can adapt to YOUR PURPOSE (which is essentially timeless and it also allows you to change your purpose in the future). This book is not about me, it is about you and how I can help you achieve your purpose with LinkedIn.

I have included some interesting stories, anecdotes and philosophical comments. I sincerely hope you find these items useful for your purpose and that they make the book a little more interesting and relevant for your situation.

I also encourage you to do things in a way that suits your personal style. I am extremely confident that you will be able to identify what will work for you — but don't be afraid to challenge yourself and experiment with some new concepts too — after all, I would like you to gain maximum value from this book!

As mentioned earlier, I also recommend that you be ethical and observe common etiquette with everything that you do on LinkedIn. To preserve the quality and integrity of the LinkedIn Platform, and its' future value for both you and LinkedIn, there are various algorithms (complex mathematical equations and processes) and spam reporting options that will detect 'bad behavior' and contraventions of the LinkedIn User Agreement http://linkedin.com/legal/user-agreement.

If this bad behavior is detected, you will run the risk of having your privileges reduced or your LinkedIn Profile removed. LinkedIn have told me that they have already deleted millions of profiles that were essentially created by either spammers or people with bad business practices.

Action 3: *Apply your action steps in your own personal style in an ethical way, abiding by LinkedIn etiquette and the LinkedIn User Agreement*

1.3 Selecting Your Purpose – Based On Your Values

This book is not a 'scripts' book. I will give you various ideas and concepts that you can adapt to your situation.

Let me explain why. Throughout my life, my purpose has changed several times based on a combination of values and circumstances. My goal in this book is to empower you by sharing the skills and knowledge I have acquired so that you can achieve your purpose. I believe that it can give you a shortcut to results – provided you take action.

I fully understand that in today's world, you need to have an income to survive. I am fortunate to have found a good balance in my life across a range of areas – family and friends, work and contribution, health and lifestyle.

I have a number of goals that I am striving to achieve, but I am also fortunate to have learned the difference between value and price.

Some of the best things in life are priceless.

Have you written your purpose on paper yet? If so, does it include a comprehensive statement about how you want to live your life?

Have you declared your career or business values?

Are you prepared to be the person you want to be rather than what the world wants you to be?

Are you a human being or simply a human doing? Is it time for you to be happy now, rather than happy when X happens?

Are you chasing what you don't have rather than valuing what you do have? Will you look back in years to come after you have got what you want – but wish you were back where you are now with what you already have? This is a very important question for busy parents with young children – I can assure you that they grow up way too fast!

Do you value good health? Do you value quality relationships? Are you putting deposits into your relationships bank account (where if you invest, you can get interest – putting in a little bit all the time will pay much higher dividends)?

Do you value giving back and sharing your knowledge and skills? When you look back in 10 years' time, will you say that you have been living according to your purpose?

There are all sorts of coaching tools (like the 'Life Success Wheel' or 'Areas of Personal Growth and Fulfillment Chart') that coaches use to help you clarify your direction at the start of the coaching process. The following table is a summary of some of the life areas you may like to think about.

When you fill in this Life Area Values and Purpose table (available FREE as an Excel Spreadsheet download when you join our 120 Ways Publishing Membership Program at http://120ways.com/members), think of values as what is important to you in this area of your life and purposes as what you would like to do or achieve in this area of your life.

Life Area	Values	Purpose
*Career, Business or Enterprise		
Community Contribution		
Creative Outlets		
Exercise or Sport		
Faith or Spirituality		
Family and Friends		
Fun and Recreation		
Health and Wellbeing		
Hobbies and Interests		
Home or Physical Environment		
Money and Finances		
Personal Development		
Personal Relationship and Romance		
Professional Advice and Support		
Social Life		

Main focus of this book

What do you really value? This is an important component of deciding on your purpose. You may say that your purpose is to reach a certain income amount per year. But what would you be willing, or not willing to do for that amount? This is where your values determine your actions.

If you say that you value time with your family, do you use various tools and techniques to make time for your family, or do you get swept up by various distractions and spend even less time with your family?

If you value relationships but you never have the time or the motivation to keep in touch, do you really value relationships? LinkedIn can assist in this area. For example, if you write a Post, some of your contacts will be notified and they will be 'reminded' that you exist. This does not avoid the responsibility you have to keep in touch with your valued family members, friends, colleagues, peers, clients and advisers in person, via email, SMS, phone or other social media or applications, but it can complement those activities.

If you value balance in your life, do you try and learn every new thing yourself or do you gather some general information so that you can understand the basics and then source an expert for some professional advice or support? This fee for service approach can save you hours in wasted time and effort. It is based on the old principle of saving cents but wasting dollars – if you are so worried about saving cents, you can potentially lose hours of time and lots of dollars from lost earnings.

For example, I was running a course on 'How to create a simple WordPress website' and one of my participants made beautiful cakes from a home kitchen. She also had a young family who were involved in a lot of after school activities. Rather than ask an IT person for some expert help, she would stay awake until all hours of the night trying to work out the technology herself (and she hated doing it).

She also told me that she loves making cakes and that they sold well. I believe that every small business owner should understand what they are paying for when they create a website, but she would have been far better off asking for some website help and having some well-earned rest in the evening – even if that meant spending more of her time making yummy cakes (which she enjoys) to pay for the website assistance!

*The most successful entrepreneurs do not do everything themselves.
But again, you must still TAKE ACTION even if you source
professional assistance. You cannot delegate everything.*

I often find that attending a course can be very helpful for gaining a general overview of a topic. You can also receive additional insights from the other course participants. Reading a book is a way you can do this in a 'self-help' way.

I truly believe that once you are clear on your purpose, one-on-one support or assistance, from a trusted, reliable and skilled professional, is far more effective and efficient in the long term.

For example, do you really want to learn how to conduct a major operation on your own body (just in case you ever need to do one) or would you rather a specialist do it for you under general anesthetic with all of the latest technology only if it is needed?

Do you really want to go through a huge learning curve to specialize in a new area, or simply pay for some professional assistance and get the job done immediately?

If you value contribution, do you simply pay an amount of money towards someone else's project via philanthropy or crowd funding or do you give your time or expertise to a group, cause or organization? A personal voluntary contribution can sometimes be far more valuable than a dollar contribution.

*Many people have told me over the years that the work they do on a
voluntary basis is far more inspiring and meaningful to them than
any of the paid work they have completed.*

At this point, I encourage you to write down, on paper (and digitally if you wish), your main purposes in life, based on your values. This is not something that needs to be set in stone for life, it is just for now and will help you make constructive choices as you read this book.

If you can't formally decide what these purposes should be, think about what is most important in your life right now (which you can easily determine by how much energy and time you currently devote to it) and what you are not prepared to give up (even if you were offered millions of dollars). Sometimes you might be able to hit the jackpot of what is most important to you by writing down what you absolutely do not want under any circumstances because this can help you to define what you do want.

You may also need to reflect on any past challenges you want to overcome in the future (for the record, I do not believe anything is insurmountable). Ultimately, you will need to decide if you or your enterprise is the right fit for an opportunity and you may need to explain certain aspects of your past so that they can join the 'right' dots together rather than the 'wrong' dots.

For example, I worked with an amazing teacher who did not have any children and she wanted to work in a school teaching young children. Although it is against local employment regulations, she was regularly asked in job interviews whether or not she had children of her own and she would reply that she didn't.

Consequently, she kept missing out on securing a job even though she had reached the final interview stage and was extremely well qualified and experienced. Instead of just saying she didn't have any children, she could have said that she doesn't have any children, but she has spent many hours interacting with her nieces and nephews, she regularly reads to them and she has been involved in some of their educational decisions in conjunction with the children's parents. This creates a completely different impression and suddenly, she becomes 'suitable' for the role rather than labelled as 'childless' and 'unsuitable.'

I would also like to mention that there are a range of purposes that you may not have realized you could achieve through LinkedIn. I am including this information because I have had a number of very reluctant clients who have protested quite strongly about whether or not they should even have a LinkedIn Profile!

How else can LinkedIn help you?

- it enables you to create a cloud based personal database so that you can keep in contact with friends, fellow students you have met through study, work colleagues, managers, advisers, stakeholders etc (particularly important if you have worked in one organisation for many years and you are about to be retrenched – try and connect with everyone before you leave!)

- it is extremely valuable as a component of your digital footprint for either your name or your enterprise name as it will be able to be search engine optimized

- it reserves online real estate so that no one else in the future can secure the same spot (if you customize your LinkedIn Public Profile URL)

- you can massage your message and create the right message for your purpose

- you can build your reputation and counteract bad publicity

- it can form part of your enterprise backlink strategy

- it can be a way to document your history for future generations and be useful for family members who may not know this information

- if it becomes too time consuming, you can change your visibility and communication settings to reduce your online exposure and number of emails

- it can give you a process to help you achieve your purpose and create a network that can sustain you in the future, particularly if you build a digital asset (or content bank) that includes both content and a substantial record of regular online activity

- other people, both friends and foes, can either be attracted or disconnected as required

- it can be a tool to complement your offline networking – you can keep the details of the people you meet in

LinkedIn rather than accumulate a pile of quickly obsolete business cards in the top drawer of your desk!

- you can utilize the power of the relationships and connections you have collected to increase your referral opportunities

Action 4: *Define your values and your purposes in life*

1.4 Learn The Skills To Achieve Your Purpose

Once you have defined your values and chosen your purposes, you will need to select the paid and free actions you need to complete to achieve success.

You also need to realize that you may need to learn some new skills to achieve your purpose and not just rely on the skills you already have to achieve your purpose. For example, most people are educated and taught how to do a job, but most people are not taught how to find a job.

This book can potentially help you in all areas of your life, but it is most relevant for your Career, Business or Enterprise Life Area. It may also help you find professionals who can assist you in your other life areas (if you complete an Advanced Search on LinkedIn).

If you are struggling, for any reason, to find the type of job or enterprise you are ultimately seeking, I believe that there are three main ways to succeed.

They are – networking, referrals and voluntary work.

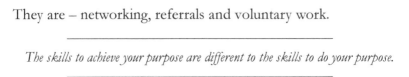

The skills to achieve your purpose are different to the skills to do your purpose.

You may be finding it difficult to achieve your purpose of finding a job due to long term unemployment, retrenchment, mental or physical health issues, your level of experience or qualifications, personal circumstances, caring responsibilities, disability, gender, ethnic background, faith, current financial resources, language ability, age etc. But these are not reasons to prevent you from pursuing your purpose.

On the path to your purpose, you will have a lot more success if you can match yourself with a person or organization that is also operating according to their purpose and that purpose just happens to be aligned with your purpose.

There is also a much greater chance of success if you are both working towards a fair exchange. You need to acknowledge that both you and the other person are acting out of self-interest (and that is not a bad thing).

In the beginning, you may wish to accept slightly more of the risk by offering a free or low-cost introduction to your value.

Let's look at several reasons why some people (referred to as 'some people' below) are not able to achieve their career purpose with traditional job search techniques:

- up to 90% of jobs are never advertised (and some people only rely on job ads)

- the most effective form of recruitment is via referral, usually from existing employees (and some people don't ask for referrals)

- the nature of work is changing very rapidly and the average duration for an individual role is now only five to seven years (and some people think that the same job will be around forever)

- voluntary work gives people an opportunity to see you without a financial commitment (and some people refuse to do any voluntary work)

- the main reason you are hired is for cultural fit, not skills (and some people fall into the trap of believing all of the 'reasons' they were given when they didn't get a job – those 'reasons' are usually just 'safe answers' so that the potential employer is not sued – if you got an interview, you were a contender up until that point!)

- diversity is increasing, but you still need to be able to share your story appropriately (and some people don't make an effort to understand the local context and describe their value appropriately)

- career management is now an individual responsibility rather than a company responsibility (and some people don't accept this responsibility and just 'go with the flow' and wonder why their career has stalled)

- technology is shifting the nature of work, but not the value of working – paid or unpaid (and some people don't adjust to this changing dynamic or see the value in unpaid work)

- up to 85% of business is sourced through referral and verification of that referral (and some people don't have a digital profile suitable for verification)

- the online world and your digital brand is used for review, assessment and due diligence checks (and some people have inappropriate content on their profiles)

- 95% of decision makers will seek digital verification before making a decision (and some people assume that reference checks will only be conducted over the telephone through listed referees)

- being proactive is important – but so is being attractive to the right opportunity – by coming up in search results and providing a compelling offer (and some people wait for everything to come to them without being proactive or making information available)

Ultimately, to overcome these challenges, anyone seeking a career, business or enterprise opportunity in modern society needs to learn attraction and referral skills – and build a network.

Nowadays, as Porter Gale suggests, "your network is your net worth." In the past, it may have been location based, but now it is electronically based.

Action 5: *Achieving your purpose in a changing market means learning attraction and referral techniques, building your network and creating a digital asset*

1.5 Aim For 80% Rather Than 100%

My favorite quote of all time is, "Occupation is the necessary basis of all enjoyment" by James Henry Leigh Hunt.

You probably know what it is like to be 'in the zone.' Where time and space don't matter anymore. Where you know and recognize that you are in your own personal groove. Where everything flows and you feel that everything is right in the world, at that moment.

In my humble opinion, it is unrealistic to expect any job, work or activity to be 100% congruent, 100% of the time.

If you fully acknowledge and appreciate your strengths, if you review the local market conditions and opportunities (based on facts, not anecdotes or attitudes from past experience or jaded friends) and you use a successful strategy to secure the most relevant work or business, then you have the amazing opportunity to be spending at least 80% of your time doing what you love.

During the 20% of your time when you are doing things that are not as congruent as the main 80%, you can remind yourself that you are very fortunate to spend most of your time in alignment with your values.

For example, there are several tasks that I need to complete that I don't enjoy to maintain my amazing lifestyle. I am not a fan of deleting junk emails and keeping up to date with general administration, but I do it so that for the rest of my time, I can do what I love!

By doing these tasks, I also have the opportunity to fully appreciate how amazing it is to live my life. You cannot see the light if you have no sense of darkness.

I don't believe it is something that you can automatically achieve, not even after reading this book and taking all of the action steps! It usually takes various stages and some time.

As I have said previously, many of us have been educated to do a job, but not educated on how to find a job. You may have been taught how to offer excellent customer assistance for a product or service but not how to sell that product or service. Perhaps you are passionate about a cause but you don't have the resources to champion that cause.

Finding the right job, for the right person, in the right enterprise (your own or someone else's – business or social), is a skill. This book will give you many new skills and strategies that you can use to be more congruent in your approach.

It is important to remember that to move forward, it is usually a process of stages – stage one, stage two, stage three etc. If you are courageous enough to take the right steps, in alignment with your values, your life will develop more quickly and it will be so much more purposeful.

"If you focus on results, you will never change.
If you focus on change, you will get results."
Jack Dixon

I have been in situations where the daily grind is just that, a daily grind. Where I could not see any way out of a particular mindset, context or circumstance. Even in the darkest moments, there were still little things that I could do to find peace and happiness. The best part was, they didn't even cost me any money!

If you have been having dark moments recently, I encourage you to look around and see the true value of what you already have. It could be the simplest of things – like being able to see, hear, walk or talk. Some people do not have these simple luxuries.

If you have been comparing yourself to others, please stop! Their journey is their journey. Your journey is your journey. Again, take action and responsibility for your outcomes. Do what you can, even if you don't have much. Take small steps in stages.

Please don't beat yourself up if you can only do a little at a time, just get started. You will gather strength along the way.

Action 6: *Achieving your purpose takes new skills – complete steps in stages to reach your 80% congruence average*

1.6 Define Your Boundaries On Your Terms

So now that I have finished my short philosophical overview of values, let's make sure you have defined your purpose.

It is important to remember that defining a purpose is not a permanent solution. It is simply a starting point. If you can create a

Sue Ellson

sort of 'guidelines boundary' this will allow you to keep your options open.

Most people shudder when I say the word 'boundary' and they have a vision of being trapped within four walls. I have lived a part of my life where there were literally no boundaries and it was impossible to do anything. I couldn't start, make a choice, say yes or say no – as I didn't have any criteria for making a decision.

When you have a boundary in your life, you have the ability to explore a range of creative opportunities within it. Instead of visualizing four straight walls, I encourage you to visualize an abstract room with numerous walls that can be rearranged into a different layout at any time.

This simply gives you a framework to work within and enables you to make choices aligned with your values. For example, I will not, under any circumstances, and no matter how much I am offered in remuneration, have anything to do with gambling or drugs.

Once you set up a framework to work within based on your values, you can start taking action steps towards your purpose. It may not be a direct line. It may require several stages. It may change along the way as you experiment and discover the ins and outs and the reality once you have a bit more experience.

Here is a quick example. I remember providing a free 15 minute career exploration chat to a mother and daughter at the Career Development Association of Australia stand at the Reinvent Your Career Expo in Sydney. The mother had been in the same role in a tertiary education college for over 30 years and was looking for something different – but she had no idea where to start.

I suggested that she try a few different options on a part time or voluntary basis first – even if it was in an area that she wasn't considering in the future. This approach would also give her an opportunity to mix things up a bit in the short term and help her change her view of her existing job and help her see how other job roles are both similar and different to her existing role.

I also encouraged her to adopt a gradual transition approach. She started making jokes about quitting her job and working part time in a canteen and it being quite dangerous as she would be handling knives – so I am guessing she must have been a little bit angry about her current situation at that time! Or perhaps she was just making a funny joke!!

Her daughter was currently working in retail banking but she knew that this wasn't the right fit, despite the fact that she was particularly good at her job. She told me that she had always wanted to fly aircraft – almost the polar opposite! A man I met many years ago was a helicopter pilot and he told me how he lost interest in his job because he was 'just a machine operator.' I told her this story and also suggested that before she leaves the bank and starts an expensive pilot training course, she could consider going on a few test flights with a flying instructor. Both mother and daughter were very excited about this suggestion, because it meant that as early as tomorrow, they could take an action step towards her purpose and move forward.

Now if the daughter buys a package of flying lessons, this will probably cost her several hundred dollars. But, it will still be an amazing experience and it will help her clarify whether or not flying aircraft is truly her purpose.

She may realize that banking, where she is actually working directly with people, may be more aligned. But she won't know that until she goes and investigates her flying options and tries it for herself. It is better, in my view, to die knowing what could have been rather than spend your whole life wondering what might have been and living with regrets.

I say this because when I was 26, I went to a 40th birthday party. I would say that at least half of the people there were complaining about their lives – their jobs, their partners and their kids. Call me naïve, but I thought at the time, if I am like that when I am 40, please shoot me! Fortunately, I am now 50 and I have never felt like this. But again, I had to take action steps to make sure I did not end up like them.

_____

So to sum up, you may or may not have found your purpose yet, even though you have bought this book. You may have some ideas and you may still be trying to finalize them.

_____

That is okay. This book will still help you, particularly if you take the time to add the details of your past story to your LinkedIn Profile. Recording those details is a process in itself and it can be enormously beneficial at clarifying the things you want to keep or not keep in your future.

Just to give you a heads up, my values, way back in my early 30's, were to focus on roles that included learning and teaching, people and technology, regular and passive income, flexible hours, some travel and having a 'fallback' position available just in case.

As you can see, this is not about selecting an 'occupation' from a long list created via a 'skills assessment.' It is about determining my values and what is important to me. That way, when an opportunity comes up (or I go looking for one), I am able to assess it in relation to my values and I am able to quickly and easily decide 'yay' or 'nay' each time. My framework boundary is now firmly in place and it has served me well for 20 years!

What is even better is that it is my framework. It incorporates my values and it has consistently helped me make good decisions.

Over time, I have appreciated, more and more, the people who do the jobs that I simply do not ever want to do – thanks to them, I can do what I love.

So please don't be afraid! By choosing to act according to your values, you are actually empowering others to do the same! You may not want to be a tram driver, but someone else may love doing this job.

Another benefit of turning 50 is that I can now live according to my values without apology (although I do insist on always living ethically and authentically with due respect for everyone else and the planet). It is one of the many benefits of growing older – and wiser!

Sometimes, you may need to work or participate in an activity based on your future goals. For example, if you are currently studying towards a particular qualification, the only work you may be able to find based on your other commitments could be something in hospitality. This role still serves your ultimate purpose and gives you transferable skills that you will be able to utilize in the future.

Never forget that no time is ever wasted! If the best time for you to complete a task was 10 years ago, don't worry. The second best time for that task (if it is still relevant), is right now!

Remember that whatever you have done in the past was based on what was happening in your life at that time. And you already know that you can't go back.

However, that experience has given you valuable lessons that you can apply today and it has developed your wisdom. It is NEVER too late to start heading in the right direction.

Having a good strategy for your future means that you have an even greater chance of reaching your goals! Once you are clear on your purpose, you will be able to achieve even more with LinkedIn.

Action 7: *No time is ever wasted – even if you are not clear on your purpose right now, start taking action and record your past for a better chance of reaching your goals in the future*

2. Pre Work Starting Points

Let's start with some important LinkedIn concepts and actions that need to be understood and completed before you can really achieve your career, business or enterprise purpose with LinkedIn.

Remember that LinkedIn was originally created as a network for professionals. Over time, it has morphed into a publishing platform after acquiring the services of SlideShare (PowerPoint presentation hosting) and Pulse (news aggregator).

It continues to acquire additional services (like Lynda for your training needs and Connectifier for cross platform individual information) and it is predicted to morph into a business to business platform in the future (and I discuss other possible options in Section 18).

A social media platform that is willing to constantly grow and adapt has a much greater chance of being sustainable in the future.

Action 8: *Remember that you need to understand the basic concepts of LinkedIn to achieve your purpose – be ready to adapt to the changes that will continue to occur*

2.1 Select The Initial Purposes You Would Like To Achieve

If you have access to the internet, you have probably enjoyed the benefits of an internet search. In fact it is so common to search for information online now that most people will tell you to 'just Google it.' Google engineers have spent countless hours updating their algorithms so that you can usually find the information you are seeking on the first page of Google Search Results.

Likewise, engineers at LinkedIn do the same. They have algorithms that prevent new users from spamming the platform (as mentioned in Section 1.2). They have algorithms that help tailor job advertisements and content for your newsfeed based on your profile, connections and activity.

They also have a range of algorithms that reward certain types of contributions or behavior. For example, if you start endorsing your connections, your details could be sent to your Connections with a suggestion that you be endorsed for your most popular skills. These algorithms can either help or hinder your performance and results from LinkedIn.

You need to remember that the algorithms are always looking for the best results from a search query. So if you want to achieve your purpose with LinkedIn, you need to determine your purpose first so that you can attract the right interest.

If you still need some help to clarify your purpose based on your values, I suggest that you ask for some professional advice from a career adviser (also called a career development practitioner, facilitator, career counsellor, career adviser, career coach etc.) that has the relevant experience, qualifications and networks for your industry or profession.

If the advisor uses a career or psychological assessment tool to help with this process, please make sure that they are formally qualified in the use of that tool and are suitably qualified to interpret the results for someone with your background.

I have previously worked with a client who had completed a $1,200 assessment with a psychologist, and this 'expert' told him that he had no future – I would like to think that this process could have given him some clues as to what he could do in the future – not just tell him that it was all hopeless!

If you are involved in a particular enterprise, it is a good idea to have one or more mentors that can share their wisdom, knowledge and networks with you so that you can develop a very clear understanding of your future direction and discover what particular techniques will be most helpful.

I also recommend that you source professional career or enterprise advice from someone who does not have a vested interest in a particular outcome or a hidden agenda that will take you in the wrong direction.

For example, if you seek free advice from a recruiter who has a job to fill, an education provider who wants you to complete more study or a welfare organization that wants you to meet a certain criteria so that they can receive further funding, this is not an adviser who is exclusively working in your best interests.

I have also written an article on 'How To Choose Your Next Job Or Career' which is online at http://linkedin.com/pulse/how-choose-your-next-job-career-sue-ellson – this gives you a simple Mind Map process that you can use to review your past and contemplate a future that is aligned with your values and your non-negotiables. You can then create your own decision framework.

Whilst your overall purpose on LinkedIn may be to reach a particular goal, there are many other components that could be a part of the overall process of achieving your purpose.

You may want to do some or all of the following:

- find a job

- build a personal or business brand

- develop a network

- maintain relationships

- source leads

- do research

- create a reputable digital footprint and build a digital asset over time

- share your knowledge

- build an enterprise – business, social or other

- increase awareness and provide advocacy

- create your own database of contacts

- scale and leverage the relationships you have developed for regular referrals

Now is the time to define your overall purpose and then choose the specific actions you need to take to achieve your purpose.

Secondly, you need to know that you can select more than one purpose! If you are interested in a portfolio approach in the future, you may have up to four purposes and you could still share this message effectively via LinkedIn.

Right now, I provide consulting services around LinkedIn to individuals and organizations, I regularly teach on the topics of websites and technology, I run various online portals of information and a whole lot more. All of these purposes are supported by LinkedIn.

However, I do not recommend that you ever consider having two LinkedIn Profiles – under any circumstance. If you already have two LinkedIn Profiles, please follow my instructions on how to delete your duplicate profile at http://linkedin.com/pulse/duplicate-linkedin-profiles-how-delete-merge-two-more-sue-ellson

Action 9: *Select your initial overall purpose and some specific purposes for LinkedIn*

2.2 Select Your Primary Keywords

If you are clear on your purpose, determining the most likely keywords for that purpose can be straightforward. However, you could fall into the common trap of using the keywords that you know and not using the keywords that your target audience would use to find you. Any keywords you choose should be in popular use by your target audience.

Let me give you an example. I spoke at the Career Development Association of Australia http://cdaa.org.au annual conference in Adelaide, South Australia and I signed in to my LinkedIn account, live from the podium. I then completed an Advanced Search and looked for a 'career counsellor' in the location of 'Adelaide.' Not one of the people in the room or in the association showed up in my search results on that day.

"Why not?" I hear you ask. Because they used the title 'Career Development Practitioner' in their LinkedIn Profiles but this was not the word used in my search (or the word that their target audience would be likely to use). Now when I do the same Advanced Search, I get a lot more results!

If you are worried because you have more than one purpose and you will have a lot of different primary keywords, don't be. As I have already mentioned, you can achieve that on LinkedIn too. You can also change directions completely (I have helped several people change into a completely different occupation – based on a close review of their values and purpose).

You can update your primary keywords at any time and you can include primary keywords from different disciplines too.

The number one space for these primary keywords is in your headline,
the box that is directly underneath your name on LinkedIn.
You have 120 characters in this location.

Some LinkedIn advisers recommend that you describe yourself in your headline rather than use keywords. I don't. Your headline does not always appear in full (usually the first 50-70 characters), but the keywords are a priority item in LinkedIn Search Results. The first part of your headline is the most important as this abbreviated title is what appears when you are listed in LinkedIn notifications.

If you were my client and I had a choice between including fancy characters and descriptive words or alternatively, another relevant keyword in your LinkedIn headline, I would nearly always go for the extra keyword, particularly if the keyword is directly aligned with your purpose and target audience.

However, the words you use in your headline still need to make some sort of logical sense and help the person reading your profile understand the value you offer. There is no significant value in repeating any word.

It can be helpful to include a 'differentiator' word – something that makes your LinkedIn Profile memorable. For example, I was working with a very senior adviser in his own practice and after we had included all of his main keywords, we added 'Believer in Serendipity.' This short phrase made his LinkedIn Profile very distinctive and it briefly highlighted the nature of his approach.

If you are not sure where to start with Primary Keywords, read the next section to find out places to source your Keywords and then choose the most valuable Keywords for your purpose as your Primary Keywords.

Action 10: *Select your Primary Keywords and include the most important keywords in your headline underneath your name (up to 120 characters)*

2.3 Select Your Secondary Keywords

Secondary keywords are designed to complement your Primary Keywords. They fall into various categories and have different purposes. Search algorithms work on multiple factors so ensuring that you have these Secondary Keywords ready will give you the best chance of coming up in search results aligned with your Primary Keywords.

As I describe these Secondary Keywords, I will give you examples related to someone who is a Senior Human Resources Generalist (primary keywords) with a range of specialties (secondary keywords).

- **Related Keywords** are words that are associated with your primary keywords. They are likely to be words that define your specialty area or niche and could be used to find you directly based on this area of expertise (e.g. Organizational Development, Change Management)

- **New Keywords** are words that replace old keywords that may have been used in the past. Every industry and profession is regularly updating their common use terms, so if you want to be viewed as 'current,' you need to be using them too (e.g. People and Culture, Talent Management)

- **Old Keywords** are words that may still be in use but they are not used as frequently as either the current keywords or new keywords. If you continue to use these and someone wants to search via that term, you may be the only person who appears in search results! (e.g. Personnel, Staffing, Workforce Development)

- **Descriptive Keywords** are directly aligned to give more definition to your primary keywords. They are also qualifying words to help the reader understand more about your skills and unique value proposition. They can also help differentiate you from other people (e.g. Senior, Certified Professional, Management Experience)

- **Positioning Keywords** these keywords help the reader say 'hell yes' or 'hell no' when they read your LinkedIn Profile. If you have a certain style or preference, be open and frank about this upfront so that the right people do contact you and the wrong people don't. Why waste time going through an unnecessary qualification process? You could have simply stated your preferences up front and saved your own time and the other person's time. Another way to think about this is to describe your ideal organization – these keywords help define the right cultural fit (e.g. Proactive, Business Focused, Inclusive, Consultative)

- **Culturally Appropriate Keywords** these keywords may need to be added or removed depending on your location. Certain cities and countries have particular expectations. Try not to make any particular assumptions about a new location without qualified advice – don't assume that because your previous location had a particular expectation, it will be the same in a future location (e.g. Willing to travel, Current Availability, Language Skills)

- **Standard Keywords** are keywords that you would always include regardless of your location, profession or industry. Just as Google wants every website to have an About Us and Contact Us page, I would suggest that certain content must always be added to your profile (e.g. Your email address or preferred methods of contact, your call to action (what you want the right people to do once they have read your profile), your reasonable calibrated special offer (you don't try and get them to spend $2,000 immediately, but a special offer for $20 could be quite okay and is a low level commitment. From there you can provide a value ladder of progressively higher commitments until you reach the full commitment – you don't want to put a trip wire in too early and miss out altogether)

What is absolutely most important when preparing your list of primary and secondary keywords is that you constantly think about the target audience you are trying to attract and what search terms they will be using to find you.

You also need to repeat your keywords, in context, frequently. Naturally, a profile with particular keywords featured frequently is more likely to come up in search results than a profile that only has the keywords mentioned a few times.

If your profile is not coming up on the first page of search results for your keywords when you do a search, then you know that your keywords are not in the best locations or repeated as often as necessary (or someone else's LinkedIn Profile is even more relevant). When you perform a search (or an advanced search), the keywords you have chosen will appear in bold on the screen and this gives you some extra clues as to where it is most important to feature your keywords.

Some people find it easy to select their secondary keywords, others need some help. You can find keywords related to your purpose by:

- reviewing selected job advertisements in your target range

- reviewing selected job descriptions and key selection criteria

- visiting job information websites (like My Future http://myfuture.edu.au or Riley Guide http://rileyguide.com)

- utilizing the Google Keyword Planner Tool http://adwords.google.com.au/KeywordPlanner

- viewing other people's LinkedIn Profiles including peers, mentors, consultants in your industry or profession

- visiting websites in the industry or profession (right click your mouse on the website page, choose 'View Page Source' to see the title, keywords and meta description in the HTML code)

- scanning magazines, publications and journals for the industry or profession

- consulting job aggregator websites that curate content from multiple locations for jobs, industries or professions (like Indeed http://indeed.com). These websites are also called career search engines, job crawlers and job spiders

Action 11: *Select your secondary keywords for your purpose*

2.4 Prepare For The Process

When you purchased this book, I am reasonably confident that you did not allocate the full amount of time you would need to complete all of the 120 actions – but if you did, bravo!

You probably had a reasonable expectation that you would find at least a few good ideas to make your investment worthwhile. As I mentioned in Section 1.1, if you can complete at least 20 actions, I am confident that you will be happy and you will see results.

To gain the most from the process of taking action, I encourage you to:

- aim to complete your minimum viable product (MVP) first – it is much better to have a 'window shop version' than a perfect LinkedIn Profile that is non-existent

- view this process as more than filling in boxes – most of my clients report that they have gained enormous value from the process of completing their LinkedIn Profile as they were reminded about their past achievements, they connected with past colleagues and they received new results almost instantly

- complete it in stages – either on your own or with a mentor or accountability partner

- reflect and review – you will discover new information in the future that could be useful so keep a notepad handy whilst you are doing the work to jot down the great ideas you have along the way (for following up later on)

"If you fail to plan, you are planning to fail!"
Benjamin Franklin

I don't want you to waste your money, I want you to get great results and start achieving your purpose with LinkedIn!

Action 12: *The process of taking action will be a huge part of your success on LinkedIn – so work on completing your minimum viable product as soon as possible*

2.5 Allocate Some Time To Achieve Your Purpose

Your current LinkedIn Profile could be at the beginner, intermediate or advanced stage (you will only get to the right stage when you are achieving your purpose and not just getting traffic but actually making conversions).

I usually suggest to people that they spend at least 10 hours completing their LinkedIn Profile after they have seen me. The color usually drains from their face in one second! Ten hours may sound like a lot of time, but I can assure you, it is absolutely worth it! Especially when you start getting results.

After your LinkedIn Profile has been completed, you need to allocate more time to be active on LinkedIn. Social media profiles require both details in a lot of boxes and regular activity to perform at their best.

To manage your time, I suggest that you do one section or item per day. Try and do it in manageable stages – perhaps start with version one first and update to version two a bit later. Online content requires regular updating, so it is a good idea to realize that the project is technically never finished. It will also require some regular maintenance.

Once your LinkedIn Profile has been completed for your purpose, I usually recommend that you spend a maximum of 20 minutes per week completing the most relevant activity for your purpose.

If you decide to publish a Post every so often (which I also recommend), that may take a little extra time (unless you are an exceptionally fast writer!).

Action 13: *Allocate around 10 hours to complete your LinkedIn Profile and up to 20 minutes per week to complete activity relevant to your purpose*

2.6 Collect Some Baseline Statistics And Backup Your Data

Before you start updating your LinkedIn Profile or start being more active on the LinkedIn Platform, there are a few details to collect.

Ideally, you can create a LinkedIn Statistics Spreadsheet to collect this data on a regular basis as most of this information is only available in 'real time' (available FREE as an Excel Spreadsheet download when you join our 120 Ways Publishing Membership Program at http://120ways.com/members).

Information	Link	Measure	Date
Views in the last 90 Days	http://linkedin.com/profile	Number	
Connections	http://linkedin.com/contacts	Number	
Saved Profile to PDF	http://linkedin.com/profile	Yes / No	
Influencers and News Following	http://linkedin.com/pulse/discover	Details & Yes / No	
Companies Following	http://linkedin.com/company/	Details & Yes / No	
Recommendations Received	http://linkedin.com/recs/received	Number	
Recommendations Given	http://linkedin.com/recs/given	Details & Number	
Endorsements	http://linkedin.com/profile	Skills & Votes	
Member Since	http://linkedin.com/settings/	Date	
Primary Email Address	http://linkedin.com/settings/	Email Address	
Other Email Address	http://linkedin.com/settings/	Email Address	
Other Email Address	http://linkedin.com/settings/	Email Address	
Groups Joined	http://linkedin.com/grp/	Details & Number of Members	
Social Selling Index	http://linkedin.com/sales/ssi	Number out of 100	

To backup your LinkedIn Profile, in the unlikely event that your content or contacts are lost, I suggest that you do the following every three months:

1. **Views in the last 90 days** – how many views have you had in the last 90 days http://linkedin.com/wvmx/profile? Write this number down in your own paper record book or in your own Spreadsheet.

   If you would like your profile to be considered 'active' you would need to aim for 100 or more views per 90 days.

2. **How many Connections do you have?** – Make a record of your number of connections and also Export them into a Microsoft Outlook CSV file so that you can open the file in a spreadsheet program (in Excel on a PC or Numbers on a Mac). Visit http://linkedin.com/contacts and click on the cog and choose 'Export LinkedIn Connections.' You need to aim for more than 60 connections as a minimum.

I encourage you to save the file with today's date back to front at the beginning of the filename (e.g. 20160223_linkedin_connections_export_microsoft_outlook.csv – this is the format for the 23rd of February 2016). This will help you easily sort and identify each version of the file you have downloaded. (You need to have your internet browser program [Google Chrome, Firefox, Safari or Internet Explorer] set to ask you where to save your downloads or move the file from your Downloads or Desktop folder and rename the file when you put it in your chosen location on your computer, cloud or USB drive).

3. **Save a copy of your LinkedIn Profile to PDF** – Always remember to save a copy of your LinkedIn Profile both before and after you make changes to your LinkedIn Profile. Do this by visiting your profile at http://linkedin.com/profile and on the screen next to the big blue box, there is a drop down arrow that links to 'Save to PDF.'

I usually save my profile as 20160223-sue-ellson-linkedin-profile.pdf (date back to front and add the words 'LinkedIn Profile'). You can also save anyone else's profile you visit in the same way (great for printing and borrowing keywords and ideas)! It is a really good idea to save all of your electronic files with dashes between words to help search tools find words in your filenames. By keeping past editions, you can see how your purpose has changed over time and if you need to re-use any past content, you have it on record.

Complete the other details mentioned in the above table. These are mostly to measure your return on investment and you simply put a new date in a new column each time you collect these statistics.

Remember, if you don't collect this data on a regular basis, you cannot find out what these results were historically.

You may also like to follow up on your invitations sent – you can do this at http://linkedin.com/people/invites

It is also a good idea to record your Social Selling Index Statistics – http://linkedin.com/sales/ssi

Action 14: *Prepare a spreadsheet for collecting your statistics, save a copy of your LinkedIn Profile to PDF and export your connections to a Microsoft Outlook CSV file. Rename and save these files in a suitable location on your electronic device or the Cloud*

2.7 Overcome Your LinkedIn Hang-ups

After working with so many people and organizations and helping them improve their LinkedIn Profiles and Activity for effective results on LinkedIn, I have discovered a range of LinkedIn Hang-ups.

Typically, most people worry about the following issues:

- who to connect to or not to connect to

- what to include or not include

- when to update a LinkedIn Profile

- what items to like, comment or share

- when to share an update

- what to write in a Post (and if you can republish something you have already written)

- where to use LinkedIn for maximum effect (phone, tablet, laptop, computer)

- how much time to spend on LinkedIn

- preferring to meet people face to face and not communicating online

- preferring not to have another online profile (particularly if they already have other online profiles that are more closely aligned with their purpose)

- why use it at all (particularly concerned about privacy)?

If you are reading this book, I trust that you are willing to learn more about these issues and make your own choices for each of these items. These items will be addressed directly in Section 17.3.

But you have to be willing to learn! Before you rule out any of the suggestions in this book, please read what I have written and the reasons for my recommendations.

You have the ultimate choice and every choice you make on LinkedIn must be aligned with your purpose. My suggestions are designed to encourage you to TAKE ACTION.

These suggestions could be different to what someone else has recommended and that's okay. I am not watching over you and making sure you do what I recommend! If you prefer someone else's suggestions, please do so – provided you understand why you are doing them and it ethically aligns with your purpose.

Wherever possible, I will give you reasons for my suggestions, because this helps you make an informed choice. If someone else suggests something different, ask them why. Then you can make an informed choice about that recommendation too!

Action 15: *Open your mind to various suggestions about LinkedIn but always make informed choices that are aligned with your purpose*

2.8 Improve Your Digital Literacy

Whether you are a digital native or a digital dinosaur or something in between, the digital world is constantly changing and evolving and you need to have a certain level of digital literacy skills to be able to communicate and operate within this marketplace.

The following suggestions will help you be more effective:

- ask yourself why you are doing something BEFORE you do it (is it really necessary for your purpose?)

- ask for help if you need it (the best in the world do)

- work with a colleague, friend, accountability partner or mentor when necessary (you will work faster!)

- limit any roadblocks to 10 minutes. If you are having any form of difficulty, stop after spending 10 minutes trying to solve the issue. Either come back later or seek some more support or information before continuing. This will save you hours and hours of your precious time (I am speaking from heaps of personal experience here!)

- don't fall for a last minute pop-up or special offer involving a payment of money (especially in a moment of frustration or weakness)

- think before you type and always proof read it before you press Save or Enter (especially if it is going to be shared with multiple people)

- complete your work in short sessions (who wants to be in front of a screen for hours?)

- take regular breaks – don't cross your legs, remember to stand up and move around regularly, drink plenty of water and enjoy healthy snacks (don't have drinks near laptops or mobile devices either!)

- educate yourself and complete the tasks associated with your new knowledge as soon as possible after you have learnt the new information (otherwise you will forget what you have learnt and lose the lesson and the benefit)

- learn enough to know what you are paying for if you seek professional advice – but take ownership of the process – you cannot necessarily delegate everything to someone else without some form of risk and you will need to do some of the work yourself (as no-one else knows your story like you do)

- persist – it can be very easy to become overwhelmed and then try to solve the issue by throwing money at the problem at a critical moment (this rarely produces a quality result because you need to supply a lot of the information for LinkedIn and the money would be better spent on final edits rather than initial compilations)

- try and understand the bigger picture – this will help you be more strategic and help you logically solve any challenges (if you get caught up in learning individual processes, you will soon realize that you can never learn all of them and they could easily change in an instant)

- review – seek feedback and analyze how things are working for you (are you getting the results you desire? If not, what do you need to do or change?)

Whilst the English language is commonly used in business, digital literacy is an essential skill for every individual in the modern world.

If for any reason you are having difficulty entering information on your LinkedIn Profile, check which version of the internet browser program you are using – for example, if it is an old version of Internet Explorer it may not work. I usually use Google Chrome on a computer or laptop. If you use the LinkedIn App, not all of the functions are available.

If you try to do profile updates on a mobile device – phone or tablet – try using LinkedIn via the internet browser rather than the App as several functions will not be available on the mobile version of LinkedIn.

Action 16: *Take personal responsibility for constantly improving your digital literacy now and in the future. Realize that you need to understand what you are doing and why you are doing it before you actually begin, or delegate it to someone else*

2.9 Familiarize Yourself With The Functions Of LinkedIn

As already mentioned in Section 2, LinkedIn started out as a professional network for members and it continues to expand and develop as a platform for publishing and business to business transactions.

I have also heard it called:

- Facebook for business (it isn't)

- A resume on steroids (it isn't exclusively this)

- Networking on steroids (it still needs your input)

- Social referral source (yes, but only if you use it well)

Some of the most well-known features that I will focus on in this book include:

- **profile** – where you can showcase your career, skills, certifications, education, publications and more http://linkedin.com/profile

- **companies** – where you can showcase your company details or find information on companies you are interested in http://linkedin.com/company

- **jobs** – where you can apply for jobs or publish job advertisements http://linkedin.com/job/home

- **groups** – where you can join like-minded individuals around topics of mutual interest http://linkedin.com/grp/

- **newsfeed** – where you can see what your connections are doing, where you can see advertisements, news from various sources and more http://linkedin.com/home

- **education** – where you can connect to your alma mater, find new education providers, source connections etc http://linkedin.com/edu

- **additional services** – these have been acquired by LinkedIn and include:

    - http://linkedin.com/pulse/ – news and posts

    - http://slideshare.net – for your PowerPoint presentations

    - http://lynda.com – online learning

    - http://connectifier.com – enhanced candidate profiling

- **additional resources** – these can help you with LinkedIn and include:

  - http://blog.linkedin.com – LinkedIn's official blog

  - http://help.linkedin.com/app/home/ – LinkedIn's help center, forum and help history section

  - http://linkedin.com/settings/ – for your personal settings

  - http://linkedin.com/wvmx/profile – who has reviewed your profile

  - http://linkedin.com/legal/user-agreement – user agreement

Some of the other LinkedIn information, products and resources will be discussed in Section 17.

Also, if you wish to live or work in a non-English speaking country, consider having your LinkedIn Profile in more than one language by visiting http://linkedin.com/profile/edit-profile-in-another-language This will create a new profile – it will not translate your existing profile so if you are not fully bilingual, think about having it professionally prepared to ensure that it represents you appropriately.

Action 17: *Login to your LinkedIn Account, review the functions of LinkedIn and select the tools that will be most useful for your purpose*

2.10 The Dangers Of Using LinkedIn Incorrectly

There are some interesting temptations and choices on LinkedIn. In the past, I have seen people struggle with being:

- too conservative and sabotaging their purpose

- too aggressive and either spamming people or ruining their reputation

- too interested in short term wins and losing long term results

- too focused on easy option tactics (like scripted sales emails) and missing effective strategies and solutions

- too manipulative and consequently appearing inauthentic and dishonest

- too willing to implement untested or unprofessional advice without discretion

- unethical

- too reluctant to apologize if they do make a mistake

You do not need to be perfect to be on LinkedIn, but like most social media platforms, it is a relatively democratic environment and bad behavior is quickly judged as poor etiquette. You must be truthful, honest and polite at all times.

LinkedIn's algorithms and reporting tools are very good at picking up bad behavior – so there is also a very good chance that your LinkedIn Profile could be deleted or suspended if you contravene their user agreement http://linkedin.com/legal/user-agreement.

I know that LinkedIn has many millions of members, but they have also deleted millions of members. As mentioned earlier, LinkedIn needs to uphold certain standards to maintain the integrity of the platform and prevent spammers from annoying genuine users.

One of the most hated LinkedIn behaviors is people who ask to connect with you via a standard rote message and then immediately email you with a standard sales message soon afterwards – I report these people immediately and delete the connection – no second chances from me!

Action 18: *Act with integrity and authenticity and work on the basis that everyone can 'win' with LinkedIn. Review the User Agreement at http://linkedin.com/legal/user-agreement*

3. Creating And Updating Your LinkedIn Profile

To access the full strength of LinkedIn, you will need to create your own LinkedIn Profile. This section helps you create or update your LinkedIn Profile for your purpose.

Let's start with an understanding of the actual process of creating and updating a LinkedIn Profile. You need to have a Purpose and then think about the Computer Experience (to attract viewers to your profile) and the User Experience (what happens when the person views your profile) and then ultimately, once you have completed your profile, you can then choose to implement the relevant strategies and tactics that will help you achieve your purpose and generate a conversion (your desired results).

Please don't panic if you don't have a perfectly clear purpose right now. You can still start the process of completing your LinkedIn Profile by documenting what you have done in the past as this may help you clarify your purpose – you will probably start to recall the things you have enjoyed and the things you didn't.

It is also a good idea to remember why you enjoyed or didn't enjoy various tasks.

For example, you could have been doing something very boring (like making coffee) but have really loved the job because you were in a great café with lovely customers and a terrific boss.

Another job may have involved you completing a task that really inspired you, but because you had a really bad boss or colleague or other issues in the workplace, you may have a negative view of the entire experience and be missing the opportunity to re-ignite that interest in your future roles.

So whilst you will start with your Purpose, to be able to attract the right viewers, you need to remember that most content online is part of a database that is part of another database etc.

Let's look at a quick example. I completed some consulting work for a local accountant who thought that he never had to have a good quality website because most of his work came via referral from someone else. He was particularly good at networking and maintaining relationships independently of social media. So I asked him, "How much work are you missing out on?" He couldn't answer the question.

Up to 85% of business comes from a referral. If someone had referred his services and that potential client had conducted a Google Search prior to contacting him, they would find very little information online to confirm his abilities (his business website does not even come up in Google Search Results)

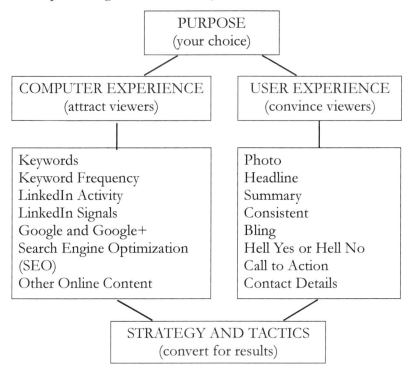

But I can tell you for a fact that his LinkedIn Profile comes up number one on page one of search results when you Google his name. This is a significant advantage of having a LinkedIn Profile – it performs extremely well in Google Search Results when a person's name is typed into a Google search query (even if you don't have a fully completed LinkedIn Profile).

Interestingly in this case, he still has not created a Company Profile on LinkedIn – but believe it or not, his Personal Profile on LinkedIn comes up number eight on the first page of Google Search Results when you search for the name of his business – so LinkedIn is helping him even more than his own website! Imagine the search results he could achieve if he created a LinkedIn Company Profile as well!

Ultimately, this local accountant needs to create a better business website, update his LinkedIn Profile and create a LinkedIn Company Profile and connect all of these via a Google+ Business Page.

At the next level of LinkedIn Optimization, I have been able to create LinkedIn Profiles that work for a person's keywords – not just their name. This means that if you are looking for an expert in a particular niche with keywords only, a person's LinkedIn Profile can appear on the first page of Google Search Results. It takes a bit more effort and some other online content collaboration – but it is possible!

Try doing a Google Search for 'independent linkedin specialist australia' and you will see what I mean! (clue – at the time of writing, it showed my LinkedIn Profile at number two on the first page of search results after my own website http://sueellson.com)

Action 19: *Create your own LinkedIn Profile based on your purpose by understanding the need to enhance the computer experience to attract the right viewers, the user experience to convince them about your offering and then choosing the most relevant strategies and tactics for achieving your purpose and generating conversions and results*

3.1 Do This Before Updating Your LinkedIn Profile

Whether you have one connection or many connections, it is a good idea to turn off the 'Notify Your Network' Option when you are about to make multiple edits to your LinkedIn Profile. This helps prevent rumors circulating about your future plans.

Sign in and visit your LinkedIn Profile page at http://linkedin. com/profile and slide the button on the right hand side of your screen to 'No, do not publish an update to my network about my profile changes.'

This can also be changed via your Settings page at http://linkedin. com/settings/ in the Privacy Controls section – select 'Turn on/off your activity broadcasts,' un-tick the box and Save your changes.

Action 20: *Turn off 'Notify Your Network' whenever you are making multiple changes to your LinkedIn Profile. Turn it back on when complete*

3.2 Essential Edit For Every LinkedIn Profile

Every LinkedIn Profile should have a customized LinkedIn Profile URL (Unique Resource Locator or address on the internet).

To do this, sign in to LinkedIn and visit your Profile page at http://linkedin.com/profile and directly underneath your photo you will see your LinkedIn Profile URL.

If you hover your mouse next to this URL, you will see a cog appear and that will take you to http://linkedin.com/profile/public-profile-settings and on the top right hand side, you can customize your Public Profile URL. (Of course, you could just go straight to this link as well!)

You cannot choose a URL that has been chosen by someone else (or even one that you have used previously). It needs to be between 5 and 30 letters or numbers, all in lower case. You cannot use spaces, symbols, or special characters. If you change it to something else, you cannot change it back. So please be CAREFUL before you change it or update it.

I am fortunate to have secured http://au.linkedin.com/in/sueellson. My exact name on LinkedIn. If you cannot choose this option, you may like to:

- add in a middle initial or name (provided it doesn't look odd as one word)

- add a number at the end (not a number related to your date of birth for security reasons)

- include a title or post nominal (like mssueellson or sueellsonbbus)

- include a keyword (not recommended unless you plan to use this keyword for the rest of your career – like sueellsonauthor)

I would also like to suggest that it is a good idea if you can reserve the same 'real estate' on other social media profiles. For example, a Twitter handle has 15 characters and I have a client who has their very common name listed as 'janetspencer10' as their identifier on LinkedIn, Twitter, Google+, Facebook etc

REMEMBER: If you customize your LinkedIn URL and then change your mind, you cannot change it back to something you had previously.

Also, if you change countries, your URL will automatically change (e.g. http://sg.linkedin.com/in/sueellson if I am in Singapore and http://au.linkedin.com/in/sueellson if I am in Australia). Keep this in mind if you are printing some business cards or have included your LinkedIn URL in your email signature. Fortunately, the old URL will still redirect to the new URL when it is typed into an internet browser.

LinkedIn also offers you the opportunity to create a LinkedIn Profile Badge that you can put in your email signature or on your website. Visit http://linkedin.com/profile/profile-badges for details.

However, I do NOT recommend this option for your email signature. I prefer to include a standard hyperlink http://au.linkedin.com/in/sueellson – because this can be read in all email programs, even those only offering plain text. If your email is printed out, people can even type in the details to their internet browser to visit your LinkedIn Profile on the spot. I also encourage my clients to include their LinkedIn URL on their resume or CV, as a decision maker can then quickly access LinkedIn and see your recommendations, full work history etc.

Action 21: *Customize your Public Profile URL and consider adding the hyperlink to your business card, resume or CV, your email signature on your phone and your email signature in your email program*

3.3 The Computer Experience – Attracting Viewers

Establishing a quality LinkedIn Profile that attracts the viewers you want for your purpose involves several components.

You need to carefully select the **primary and secondary keywords** for your niche. It also involves repeating those **keywords frequently**. To maintain relevance in LinkedIn or Google Search Results, it also requires you to be active on LinkedIn and give little clues via LinkedIn **Signals** (behavior that triggers off better search results – like connecting with a lot of people in the same industry or profession).

I have already discussed keywords in Section 2.2 and 2.3. What you choose to do in terms of activity on LinkedIn will depend on your purpose – but if you would like to think of an analogy, think of a performer who constantly spins plates on the top of poles. To keep your interest, the performer has to keep moving around, changing the scene, create anticipation and worry that something could happen so that they can keep your attention etc. Your attention is based on the value you are receiving.

The good news is that LinkedIn algorithms will keep some of those proverbial plates spinning on your behalf – and they will spin even more if you do a few extra things on a regular basis.

To really top off the Computer Experience, if you really want to maximize the results from your LinkedIn Profile, you should aim to increase your digital footprint online so that more information about you appears in **Google** Search Results. I believe it is also vital for every person and business to have a Google+ Profile (so you can personally tell Google where to find you by sharing links in your Google+ Profile and Updates) and ultimately, every person should consider having their own website (like I have at http://sueellson. com).

Even if you don't want to have your own website right now, register your Domain Name immediately so that Google will be able to recognize it as starting from today. I have my domain names registered with Crazy Domains http://bit.ly/crazydomainssueellson and have my website hosting through Bluehost http://bluehost. com/track/sueellson/ (these links are affiliate links, not reseller links – I will not receive any of your details if you click on them but I may receive a referral amount – that said, I only recommend what I personally use myself!).

I have also purchased the domain names of my children and I regularly joke that they will have to pay me a lot of money to get them back!

Once you have your own website online, make sure you add it to the Internet Archive Wayback Machine at http://archive.org/web/ – they will then add your website as it is right now and regularly index it in the future. If by some unfortunate accident you 'lose' your website, you can go here and collect a 'backup version.' I have used this website many times in the past and I encourage you to also consider giving them a financial contribution for this service at http://archive.org/donate/

Mastering the art of **Search Engine Optimization** (SEO) is quite a skill. The most important thing to remember is that you must be focused and authentic – do not try and manipulate the system with 'black hat' SEO techniques – most platforms identify these techniques quickly and penalize the perpetrators. For example, if you were an expert in Java Script, you would never put in your LinkedIn Profile headline – Java, Java, Java, Java, Java, Java, Java, Java, Java, Java, Java etc.

A LinkedIn Profile that is well optimized and meets the needs of the viewer is likely to have a lower Bounce Rate and a higher Conversion Rate.

You can reduce your Bounce Rate (the time before someone leaves your LinkedIn Profile and goes somewhere else) if they visit your LinkedIn Profile and read it for more than one minute (so please try and make your content interesting!).

You can increase your Conversion Rate if the viewer completes a relevant action (like calling your telephone number or visiting your website) or does what you want them to and that is aligned with your purpose.

You may also want to turn off 'Viewers of this Profile also viewed' because a viewer may be distracted and go to someone else's LinkedIn Profile (do this by going to Settings http://linkedin.com/settings, and un-ticking the box for "Show/hide 'Viewers of this profile also viewed' box" and Save the changes).

If you are a member of a professional association (which I highly recommend), some of the association websites offer a 'profile page' on their website as part of their Membership Program – so you can link to this online profile page in your LinkedIn Profile (under Contact Information, Websites). This article also provides a lot more tips http://linkedin.com/pulse/20141016095333-77832-how-to-showcase-your-professional-membership-on-linkedin (it is regularly revised and updated).

This Websites section in your 'Contact Info' part of your LinkedIn Profile allows you to add three websites and I encourage you to add in three if you possibly can. If you do not have your own website and you are not a member of a professional association, you could link to an enterprise website (for example, where you work) or a blog that has content related to your purpose that inspires you (the search algorithms will see this as a relevant link). You might be a member of a well-known football team and linking to that may also help people understand who you are and what interests you.

Other **online content**, written by you, can be published on LinkedIn via Posts http://linkedin.com/pulse/article/new, blogs, news sites, niche portals, relevant forums, social media etc. You need to determine what will work best for your purpose.

I can tell you, from bitter painful experience, that some websites are far more beneficial for your purpose than others and will secure a much better reach or conversion than others. For example, I have found that I can make a LinkedIn Post rank in Google Search Results better than an article on a well-known blog in my own country. To do that, I have to choose a relevant title, use markup throughout the post (see Section 4.1) and make the article sticky (people must stay on it for a reasonable length of time and click through to relevant links and like, comment or share it).

Whatever you do, make sure you post a link to any content that includes you in it on Google+ http://plus.google.com so that you can 'tell' Google to index the article so that it will appear in Google Search Results. For example, I have a Google+ Page at https://plus.google.com/+Sueellson2 (where you can also review my work at https://plus.google.com/+Sueellson2/?review=1) and this is where I share posts that can be viewed by the public or people in my Circles.

My Google+ Personal Profile is at https://plus.google.com/+Sueellson1 and this is where, in the details section, I have told Google where I am online – on LinkedIn, Facebook, Twitter, Other Websites etc. This helps all of my most relevant content appear on the first page of Google Search Results.

This is a very good risk mitigation strategy. I once worked with a corporate adviser who had spent time in jail for white collar crime. He believes this experience has helped him in his career and he needs to disclose this information to secure work now, but as you can imagine, when you search for him in Google, all of his 'bad press' has the potential to appear before his LinkedIn Profile or business website.

After helping him modify his LinkedIn Profile, his LinkedIn Profile started to appear on the first page of Google Search Results (number two) and by updating his Google+ Profile, he increased the quality of his first page Google Search Results and reduced some of the worst links to 'page two' of Google Search Results (where some people claim they hide dead bodies because so few people look on page two of Google Search Results nowadays – unless they are doing some good quality due diligence).

Did you know that you can also increase the amount of screen real estate you have in a LinkedIn Search Result? If someone completes a LinkedIn Search and the keywords they use are mentioned in multiple sections of your LinkedIn Profile, LinkedIn will highlight the major instances on the search results page.

For example, if you had the words 'Mechanical Engineer' mentioned in your headline, current job title, past job title, education, summary and experience sections, then all of these instances would be bolded in the LinkedIn Search Result. That is why I encourage you to put your most important Primary Keywords in these positions. If someone else only mentions 'Mechanical Engineer' in their headline, they will have a lot less screen real estate.

Ultimately, your goal is to make sure that if you want to achieve your purpose with LinkedIn, you need to attract the right viewers to your LinkedIn Profile (or LinkedIn Company Profile) by creating the best computer experience.

Action 22: *Understand the importance of the Computer Experience to attract viewers to your LinkedIn Profile by using keywords and SEO techniques, by being active and utilizing Signals and maximizing it even further by creating other online content and connecting it all with a Google+ Profile*

3.4 The User Experience – Convince Viewers

In Sections 2.2 and 2.3 of this book, I have discussed Primary and Secondary Keywords. As I mentioned in the previous section, the Primary Keywords need to be included in your:

1. Headline

2. Current Job Title

3. Past Job Title

4. Education

5. Summary

6. Experience

My experience has shown that these are the main fields chosen from the LinkedIn Search Algorithm to help people find someone with your expertise. They are also listed in the highest priority order. This may change in the future and other sections of your LinkedIn Profile can also include your Primary and Secondary Keywords, but as a minimum, I would suggest that you make every effort to include your most important keywords in these sections.

Further to this, I will provide some extra recommendations for each item.

- **Headline** – some LinkedIn Trainers suggest that you include special characters like √ | • in your headline. Personally, I am not a fan because I would rather use the 120 character allocation for your keywords. I sometimes even leave out commas if my client's purpose is more important than commas. Be careful if you use a slash / with a word either side of the slash e.g. Founder/Director. By not putting a space either side of the slash, the words are joined together for search purposes and you will lose the value of both words – the two words essentially become one word e.g. FounderDirector

- **Current Job Title** – you may wonder how you can add a keyword here if you are simply a 'Manager' but what you can say is 'Manager – Human Resources, Organizational Development, Change Management' as long as you make it less than a total of 100 characters. Visually, this text on the screen will also be bold so it stands out and ranks higher in SEO terms because it is 'marked up'

- **Past Job Title** – this is also very valuable as you can collect 'years of experience' by adding your keywords in to past roles. I have one job on my profile that lasted over 11 years, but only two of those years were spent 'training' and the training role started five years in – but thanks to the algorithm, my 'training' keyword has collected 11 years of value! Visually, this text on the screen will also be bold so it stands out and ranks higher in SEO terms because it is 'marked up'

- **Education** – in this section I encourage you to provide a brief description of your educational institution and list all of the subjects that were included in your qualification up to 2,000 characters. If there were many subjects, list them in alphabetical order. Also, if the subject title does not include your keywords, you may like to add at the bottom – 'various subjects in this qualification included the topics of x, y, z' (if you have enough characters remaining). You do not need to include your grades for each subject – they do not offer any keyword value

- **Summary** – your photo, headline and summary are the three sections most likely to be viewed by a visitor to your profile, and they provide a current statement of where you are at, so obviously, it is essential for you to include your keywords here. Instead of writing long sentences, I encourage you to use either dot points or very short sentences up to a total maximum of 2,000 characters. I prefer to use 'third person' language because I want the reader to remember that they are reading about Sue – if I use 'I' then they will be thinking about themselves (I can still be used if you prefer, provided you do not use it too often). Other people prefer to use the first person because they believe it is more personal and appropriate when the actual person has written the content. Alternatively you could use 'no person' and just state information without any reference to I, my, he or she

- **Experience** – I have a particular format that I like to use in the Experience Section. It starts with providing a brief description of the organisation you have worked for (even if it is well known), then a list of tasks (which

can be knowledge, skills or techniques based), then a
list of achievements and finally the URL address of the
organisation in plain text (and contact details if relevant).
This provides a standard framework that most people
understand quite easily and for those short on time, allows
them to view 'achievements' very easily – especially when
most recruiters have been taught that 'past behavior
predicts future behavior.' The good news is that although
this box only allows you to enter plain text, if you type in
a website address and view the profile on a mobile phone,
the listed link will be clickable

- **Contact details** – Unless you have a criminal record,
  celebrity status or a job requiring a high level security
  clearance, I would suggest that you include your contact
  information on your LinkedIn Profile. The reality is that
  nowadays, in most countries, there are multiple ways for
  people to find out your address and phone number –
  including the telephone directory.

  - If your LinkedIn Profile text tells the right story, you
    will eliminate the time wasters and not receive unwanted
    contact. If you are approached too often, you can
    remove your contact information.

  - If you are concerned about providing your contact
    details, only include your email address (but don't write
    it out in full otherwise the spam robots will find it
    and constantly bombard you). I like to write mine as
    sueellson @ sueellson.com (you just have to remove the
    spaces either side of "@" to make it work). If you are
    very high profile, you could provide a link to an email
    form so that if the person REALLY wants to reach
    you, they will need to jump through a few hoops and
    answer some questions directly before they hit send on
    the scripted email form! Alternatively, you could provide
    the email address of your Manager or Representative.

- **Additional sections** – Certifications, Publications,
  Languages, Projects, Volunteer, Skills and Endorsements,
  Additional Info (Interests), Advice for Contacting,
  Organizations, Honors and Awards, Test Scores, Courses

and Patents should all be completed if you have any information to include in these sections.

- The only section that I do not recommend completing is the Personal Details section – your date of birth and marital status are not necessary to share (and can potentially be used to forge your identity).

- I encourage you to provide your Instant Messaging details (IM in the Contact Info section) – for example, your Skype or WeChat information – this opens you up to contact from interstate or overseas – even local jobs sometimes require a video call from another location.

It is also important to include your location details in the Address Box in the Contact Info section. Some recruiters will not consider you for a position if you live too far away from the enterprise.

If you are willing to travel across town, you may therefore wish to mention your city rather than your suburb and you may also decide not to include your suburb if it is perceived negatively in any way (too far from transport, poor neighborhood, regularly in the news etc). Your location box under the Headline is one of the most important search fields on your LinkedIn Profile – most people will not want to find a dentist in London if they live in Paris!

I will discuss how some of these individual sections can be maximized in other sections of the book, particularly in relation to job seeking, career development and branding.

You need to add your name and according to the LinkedIn User Agreement, you are not meant to include your post nominals or other words or numbers here (but some people still do). Some women choose to include a maiden name in that field.

As a minimum, remember to list any professional membership status you have in Certifications and always put the language you need in the country you want to work in first on the list (even if it is not your native language).

Describe your projects in a consistent format (remembering once again that recruiters are taught that past behavior predicts future behavior and that by writing these details in your profile, you will be better prepared for interviews). Provide details of the voluntary work you do or have completed.

Select Skills from the suggested list where possible and sort them into your Purpose Order – from highest to lowest (with the top 10 being the most important) – consider removing any that do not serve your purpose. You can list up to 50 skills, but only do this if your purpose has you specializing in a range of areas. If you want to focus in a particular niche area, I would recommend listing up to 20 skills (and aiming for at least 20 endorsements for each Skill).

Your interests can include your personal interests and your keywords (separated by commas) and I definitely encourage you to include a call to action and your contact details in the Advice for Contacting Section.

Organizations that you belong to (or pay a membership fee to) can also be profiled. Don't forget to provide details in the 'Opportunities you are looking for,' 'Causes you care about' and 'Organizations you support' sections. When typing in the 'Organizations you support,' see if you can select the organization's company profile from the list if they have one. In the Organizations section, make sure you type in the URL in the Additional Notes box.

Congratulations if you have received any Honors or Awards! When recording this, please remember to describe the Honor or Award in a bit more detail so that someone who has never heard about it can understand the significance of the award and why you were recognized.

Try not to be bashful when describing your past and remember to use your keywords. If you don't tell, then you can't sell. If you meet a person face to face, you can anticipate what else they may need to know, but if they are looking at you on a computer screen, the only information they have is what is on the computer screen!

In some countries, boasting is not helpful, so to err on the side of caution, simply state the facts rather than embellish the description with superfluous adjectives.

If you have a really good keyword strategy, you may be able to have your LinkedIn Profile come up in Google Search Results for your keywords as well as your name – then you really know that you have search engine optimized your LinkedIn Profile!

I encourage you to do some searches on Google before you optimize your LinkedIn Profile and take a screen shot of the Google Search Results (I do this via a Google Chrome Extension called Full Page Screen Capture https://chrome.google.com/webstore/detail/full-page-screen-capture/fdpohaocaechififmbbbbbknoalclacl)

If you save this image with the date back to front at the beginning of the file name and you keep doing this over a few months, you can keep working to optimize your LinkedIn Profile for your keywords. When you conduct these searches, please sign out of Google (or Gmail) when you do it because Google track your search results whilst you are logged in. If you want to make absolutely sure you are ranking for your keywords, try doing a Google search on someone else's computer or mobile device.

If you want some more general ideas on what to put in each section, feel free to have a look at my LinkedIn Profile http://au.linkedin.com/in/sueellson as often as you like and borrow as many ideas as you wish!

Action 23: *Place your primary and secondary keywords throughout your profile, but most importantly, place the primary keywords in the headline, current and past job titles, education, summary and experience sections*

3.5 LinkedIn Strategy And Tactics – Convert For Results

You may have noticed that when a big news story breaks on the internet and you type that search query into the Google search box, a major newspaper, internet portal or news service website will usually appear first in your Google Search Results.

Why? Because those websites are regularly updating their content so naturally the Google robot scans these websites regularly and indexes their content well before a website that has not been updated in six months.

Likewise, if you created your LinkedIn Profile some years ago and haven't updated it for a while because you haven't needed a new job or enterprise opportunity, then naturally the currency of your profile will not be as high as the person who is regularly active on LinkedIn.

You also need to ensure that you have completed as many sections as possible in your profile. The only sections I haven't completed are Patents and Personal Details – Patents because I don't have any and Personal Details because it is not relevant for my purpose. However, it could be useful to mention 'Single' if you are single and interested in a role in another location.

Beyond a regular review and updating of your content, you also need to send the right 'signals' to the digital algorithms (both LinkedIn and Google). Signals are a little more complex. You have a wide variety to choose from and you can select a variety of these depending on your purpose. They can include things like:

- How often you login and what you do when you are logged in – which Posts are you looking at, liking, commenting on and sharing – are they Posts of a similar topic or from specific connections etc

- How regularly you invite people to connect with you and the rate of acceptance of those invitations

- Whether or not people like, comment or share content (and the ratios)

- Whether or not you look at the LinkedIn Profile of the author of Posts or the associated links and how long you spend there

- The quality of the external links (in either your websites section or your Posts)

- Processes you complete (like writing or receiving recommendations, providing or receiving endorsements, Posts you add, Updates you share)

- How many times you visit a LinkedIn Profile or link and the specifications of that Profile or link

- The relativity of your search queries and connections (When I connected to people in the automotive industry, my news feed content started including details of car batteries)

- The level of activity and currency of the content supplier (good quality content on LinkedIn has a very good chance of coming up in Google Search Results)

- The consistency of your activity – remember if you are logged in to Google or Gmail when you do searches, they are tracking everything!

- How long people spend on a link when they click on it or go back to search results

To have a greater chance of achieving your purpose, think about the signals that are around now and in the future that will give clues to the algorithms to help you come up in search results.

If you identify another person who is really kicking goals on LinkedIn (related to your purpose), visit their profile and then view their recent activity (drop down choice from the blue box on the screen) and look at the signals they are sending.

Don't forget that you can also develop and maintain your network of relationships through LinkedIn. Remembering throughout your life to connect with people you meet or work with will enable you to complete a certain amount of 'automatic' connection maintenance.

For example, if they see an update from you in either their Notifications or Newsfeed, they will be 'reminded' that you are still around.

Alternatively, you can pro-actively choose to nominate some of your Connections as 'VIP's' via the Tag facility. To do this, visit the person's LinkedIn Profile and click on the 'Relationship' tab and then Tag. Choose Add New Tag and call it 'VIP.'

You can even go to the next level and set up a Reminder to contact them on a periodic basis (I would suggest three times a year for your most helpful Connections).

If you have a lot of Connections and have not tagged everyone up until now, it can take some time to do the retrofit!

Remember that even if you do Tag everyone and you want to email message all of those people at the same time, you can only send an email to 50 people at once via LinkedIn and if anyone responds to that message, it goes to the other 49 people at the same time.

Action 24: *Identify the best strategies and techniques you can use to achieve your purpose on LinkedIn*

4. Performance Power Tools

Once your LinkedIn Profile has been created, it is time to decide on the tools you will use to achieve your purpose – in the short, medium and long term. LinkedIn Profiles that are fully completed (all of the sections) are up to 40 times more likely to come up in LinkedIn Search Results (that should be a good enough reason to complete your LinkedIn Profile!!).

When you are clear on your purpose, you can select an overall strategy and these tools are simply the tactics you will implement. I encourage you to select a mix of techniques to spread your risk and reward.

Action 25: *Select the tools you will use to achieve your purpose over the short, medium and long term*

4.1 Post On LinkedIn

In April 2013, LinkedIn acquired the newsreader service Pulse for approximately USD90 million. This was a game changer for LinkedIn. It moved the LinkedIn Platform from being a network for professionals to a publishing powerhouse. Some people have actually called LinkedIn a Content Marketing Platform.

Increasing the size of your digital footprint and the quality of your digital asset is achievable through LinkedIn. What I particularly like about writing Posts on LinkedIn is that they can be indexed by Google and come up in Google Search Results for your primary and/ or secondary keywords. External links can be included in your Posts but these are 'no follows' with Google (which means that the Google Indexing Robot does not go through to the other websites) so they will not aid your personal or business website backlink strategy.

Your Posts need to include a call to action with a clear value proposition. Statistics and facts are worth including. Posts can be used to encourage discussion if you ask questions and 'listicles' (how to articles) are quite popular.

Human stories are received better than brand stories and emotional language can be helpful (why not consider using some hypnotic language and power words that drive action).

If you can, make your articles scan-friendly – so if the person doesn't feel like reading all of the text, they can scan for a quick overview (use headings, white space, quotes etc). Write about what you know, in a unique way. If possible, write frequently.

Former journalists are often very good at writing catchy headlines. Content that includes a video usually has a much higher level of engagement. Offer rational assets – with emotional benefits!

Avoid anything to do with the most common sources of spam – pills, porn and poker!

I would also suggest that you remember that a lot of people read content on a mobile phone or tablet – so for this reason, break up paragraphs – I normally have a maximum of two sentences per paragraph. If you make your content easy to read here, they can 'buy' immediately – more and more internet revenue is coming from mobile devices (which is probably why Google insists that websites be mobile-friendly (responsive) nowadays.

Once you have posted two or more Posts on LinkedIn, you will have an 'author' page. Mine is at http://linkedin.com/today/author/77832 and this also tells you my Membership Number on LinkedIn – I am the 77, 832nd member of LinkedIn.

There are a few principles you need to keep in mind:

- **Post titles** – you can use up to 100 characters in your Post title, however, I recommend that you try and 'tell your story' in the first 40 characters as this is what is included in the brief details on your profile page. Try and include your chosen keywords. If you can do some quick Google searches around your proposed Post title, you may find that there is either a lot of competition or not much competition for your Post title (this can help you maximize your chance of having the Post come up in Google Search Results)

  For example, I wrote a Post that is about showcasing your professional membership on LinkedIn. If you Google 'professional membership LinkedIn' it currently comes up number one on page one of Google Search Results. This is for a number of reasons. It is published on a reputable website, it links to other relevant items on high profile websites (including LinkedIn) and people may click on those links, people obviously spend a long time reviewing the article and perhaps even bookmark it and so on (great signals to Google that it is relevant content)

- **Use markup** – there are a variety of components you can add to your Post. Different Headings (I always recommend one Heading One, several Heading Two's etc), Quotes, Bold Text, Dot Points, put some keywords near the end in bold, Add three keywords from LinkedIn at the end etc. Use all of these markup options effectively around your keywords to search engine optimize your content

- **Use links** – Google likes content that includes links – links within a website (intralinks), links to other websites (external links) and reciprocal links (backlinks where you link to someone else and they link to you). If these links are to related content on reputable websites, that is even better. You can either highlight your keywords and then link to the other website or if your article is likely to be printed on paper, you may choose to include the link URL (e.g. http://sueellson.com instead of Sue Ellson)

- **Use rich media** – include images (your own if possible – not just stock images – and consider adding a text overlay), videos, presentations, tweets, podcasts, polls, charts etc. in your Post for even more impact. If possible, rename these files using descriptive keywords separated by dashes so that even the file name can assist you with search engine optimization (for example, resize the image to the dimensions needed – currently 700 x 400 pixels for a Post on LinkedIn and I would suggest at least 400 pixels wide for an Update – and call it something descriptive which includes both the content of the image and the title of the content you are writing about – like red-fire-truck-small-business-warning-signs.jpg – this filename describes what is in the image and provides search engine optimization for the title of the article 'Small Business Warning Signs')

- **Consider long form content** – technically, you could write a Post of one sentence with a link – but, that is unlikely to generate a good response from your readers or search results. You can include up to 40,000 characters in a blog Post on LinkedIn (I usually always write more than 1,500 words and apparently Posts that are around 2,000 words perform particularly well). If you want to align your Post with your purpose, incorporate your primary and secondary keywords but always consider the reader when writing your content (don't make it so keyword rich that it doesn't make any logical sense)

- **Make it easy to read** – break up long paragraphs (in most cases, I never use more than two sentences per paragraph). Make sure you don't have any spelling or grammar mistakes. Use dot points rather than long sentences (as many people will only be scanning your content). Avoid using full stops at the end of dot points as it tells the reader to 'stop' rather than keep going. Mix up the formatting, the rich media and the text layout

- **Include a call to action** – what is the point of producing good quality content if you don't suggest what the reader can do at the end? You need to provide specific ideas – please like or share, please contact, please review my other Posts at http://linkedin.com/today/author/77832 please subscribe to my mailing list, please ask me a question, please comment and tell me what you think or tell me about your experience etc.

- **Create a Posting schedule** – as I find it fairly easy to write, I try and publish a new Post once a month. For other people, I suggest three Posts per year. As mentioned above, once you have two or more Posts, you will have an 'author' link http://linkedin.com/today/author/77832 and this enables you to link to all of your Posts in one spot and it can also be a reciprocal link you list on your own website

- **Personally respond to all comments** – it would be nice to be able to personally acknowledge all likes, but most people simply don't have the time. However, it is very important that you try and respond to all comments added to your Posts (even if you just like the comment). If you do it in a timely fashion (the same day if possible), then that is another great signal that the content and the contributor are both genuine. If a comment is negative, acknowledge the concern politely and constructively at all times. Avoid public confrontation, it is better to contact the person directly and sort it out privately and then include a closing remark rather than broadcast an argument live online

- **Review your analytics** – once you start Posting, it is a good idea to review who is reading your Posts and which ones are more popular and analyzing why. Review your analytics online at http://linkedin.com/pulse/author/analytics and adjust your strategy accordingly.

Action 26: *Add three or more Posts per year to your LinkedIn Profile and do your best to search engine optimize your content with your primary and secondary keywords and other signals*

4.2 Join Relevant Groups On LinkedIn

Groups are established by individuals or organizations to essentially bring people together around a particular theme, topic, profession, industry, association etc. An administrator needs to set it up and various managers can also be involved to help run the group. Again, you need to think about your purpose before deciding on which groups to join. When you are a member of a group, unless you turn off notifications, you will be advised when a new discussion occurs.

- **Group statistics** – is the group you are interested in a good reflection of your overall purpose? Do they have a reasonable number of group members, activity or quality discussions? Are the discussions moderated appropriately?

- **Group value** – will participating in the group increase your brand, knowledge or networks? What will you be able to contribute and what will you learn? How will this benefit your purpose but also the purpose of the group? Remember that givers gain. Also remember that posting a Like or a Comment in a Group can give you an opportunity to appear in the Group Members' Newsfeeds.

- **Group profile and relevance** – most groups require administrator approval before you can join. Quality groups can improve your profile and your presence in the online world. Please be respectful and follow the Group etiquette and guidelines for the Group you are joining (some do not allow links to be posted within the Group). Consider joining the Groups of relevant professional associations (even if you are not a paying member – but I do encourage you to be a paying member). You could also consider a local business group, an academic group, an industry group or a peer group. You can join a maximum of 65 Groups but a more realistic number would be around 15.

- **Group keywords** – remember that once again, the Group description and discussions will have keywords that are either congruent or not congruent with your purpose. Be selective and if you have an interest that is not directly aligned to your overall purpose with LinkedIn, you can still join the Group but hide the visibility of the Group logo from your profile – change your settings at http://linkedin.com/anet?dispSortAnets or via the cog at http://linkedin.com/groups/

- **Group behavior** – just as you would with your Posts, make sure you respond to written replies and be willing to acknowledge good content with a like or comment. You may choose to contact a discussion leader for further information – anyone who takes the time out to do this is likely to receive a good response. Do not post negative or hurtful comments or spam groups with sales messages – this is very bad etiquette and it will do you more harm than good. Don't just lurk and observe but not contribute. Start discussions and periodically, ask a question, respond to questions, share useful information and be a 'go-to person.' Share other people's good quality content, connect and follow influencers and fill your posts with 'stats and facts'

If you are a subject matter expert, selecting and participating in groups can be an excellent way to keep up to date with your profession or industry. It can help you build your network within that sphere and create a presence outside of your current role (which is a great back up plan). Remember to always add value and do not sell. Inform, educate and comment wisely. Recognize other people's good quality contributions. Most people I know like receiving a thank you every so often.

Action 27: *Decide on your Groups strategy for your purpose and join relevant groups and participate appropriately*

4.3 Follow Relevant Companies On LinkedIn

LinkedIn allows individuals to have Personal Profiles and organizations or enterprises to have a Company Page. It is against the LinkedIn User Agreement to have a company listed as a Person (even though that is tempting because it helps keep the Company's Connections together in one spot rather than with the individual people who are part of the Company).

Company Pages need to be established by a person who has a Company email address. For example, you cannot use a Gmail email address to create a Company Page. I recommend that all Company Pages have more than one manager so that various people can update the Company Page as required.

Company Pages allow you to build brand awareness, announce career opportunities and promote your products and services – but it is still best to do this in an informative manner rather than a sales manner.

If you do not have a company of your own, you may either work for a company, be interested in working for a company or be interested in a company because of your past or future. For this reason, you may want to follow particular companies.

It is a well-known fact that large companies using the LinkedIn Recruitment Tools are more interested in candidates that are already following their company when they apply for a role. By following companies in your particular profession or industry, you are again signaling that this is your area of preference and you are sending clues about your purpose. The more like-minded content attached to your LinkedIn Profile, the more likely you are to come up in search results..

People viewing your profile will also make certain inferences about you. If you are following the innovators in your industry or profession, you are again signaling your awareness. If you overdo it, you may look desperate. Be reasonably selective.

To go the extra mile, don't just follow your chosen companies. On an occasional basis, look at their updates and like, comment or share an appropriate update after you have read the update in full. You can see these company updates either in your newsfeed http://linkedin.com/home, from your Companies page http://linkedin.com/company/home or by visiting the individual Company's page.

When you start following a company, you can also see who else is associated with that company – other connections of yours (first degree connections), second degree connections (people connected to your connections) and employees. This could also be a valuable connection, networking or research tool for you to explore.

If you are self-employed or have your own business, make sure you create a Company Profile so that when you list your role in the 'Experience' section of your LinkedIn Profile, if you added a logo to your Company Profile, this logo will be available on your LinkedIn Profile (provided you type in the Company Page Name correctly and select it from the drop down list on your own LinkedIn Profile). This will improve your online company branding profile on both your Personal Linked Profile and your Company Page (good Company Pages are likely to come up in Google Search Results).

To review which companies you are currently following, go to http://linkedin.com/company/home

It is a good idea to review this link semi-frequently so that you can stay up to date with the news released by the companies you are following (in other words, don't just review your personal news feed at http://linkedin.com/home, for targeted content in the business world from the companies you are following, take this shortcut http://linkedin.com/company/home).

Action 28: *Decide upon your Company Pages strategy for your purpose and follow and interact with updates appropriately and then implement your networking, research and branding strategy accordingly*

4.4 Maximise Your Education

I often find that one of the most neglected sections of a LinkedIn Profile is the Education Section. Clients without a formal education worry about not having something reputable to add and clients with a formal education often do not share the details of their completed subjects, topic specialties or unique benefits derived from the educational facility.

I believe that every item listed in the Education Section, should briefly describe the educational institution (very useful for people who have never heard of it), include all of the subjects you have completed (excellent keywords) and provide a website link to the institution (great for search engine optimization for you and the institution). By entering the website link, the viewer can also contact the institution and confirm that you have received the qualification.

When you enter these details on your LinkedIn Profile, you can start typing the name of the Educational Institution and if they have a University Profile on LinkedIn, it will appear in a drop down list and you will need to select this profile (use the new name if they have changed their name since you attended). This process will register you on their alumni list and this is enormously beneficial for both you and the educational institution.

Many educational institutions that have a University Profile (for example my Alma Mater, the University of South Australia http://linkedin.com/edu/school?id=10248) also have a Company Page you can follow (for example http://linkedin.com/company/10761) or an Alumni Group you can join (for example http://linkedin.com/groups/90867). Look for these too and if it is useful for your purpose, do all three actions; list the university in your Education Section, follow the Company and join the Group. These alumni networks can be very beneficial for speaking or career opportunities.

You may also like to maximize your Education Section in a slightly different way. If you have not completed formal studies for some time (or at all), you may have completed some vocational training, some professional development or individual tuition. Why not consider adding this to your Education Section?

You don't need to limit yourself to formal education. It quite often adds relevant keywords in one of your most highly ranked sections (Education), it is a more recent update by date and it shows that you are interested in constantly learning. I would also add that you probably should have spent more than one day completing this education for it to be seen as beneficial and relevant in the mind of the person viewing your profile.

Other sections closely related to Education are the Courses and Test Scores sections. Courses are aligned with particular roles (Experience) you have had in the past and they do not provide quite as much detail as the Education Section – so as a general rule, I put most Course information in the Education Section (particularly if the content of the course is related to your primary keywords), but I always try and have at least one course added in the Course section.

The Test Scores section provides a bit more scope and is also worth completing. When you realize that the LinkedIn algorithm likes to see as many sections of your LinkedIn Profile completed as possible, the Education, Courses and Test Scores sections can provide you with some quick wins and are very easy to complete.

Action 29: *Provide comprehensive details in your Education section on your LinkedIn Profile and remain connected to your various Alma Mater Educational Institutions by selecting their details when completing your LinkedIn Profile, following their Company Page and joining their Alumni Group (if available)*

4.5 Select Your Influencers (Following)

The LinkedIn Pulse service recommends people and organizations you may like to follow based on your LinkedIn Profile, activity and signals. Visit http://linkedin.com/pulse/discover to see what they suggest.

This link also suggests key Influencers you can follow (the top 300 or so people hand-picked by LinkedIn because of the great content they share). Once again, this service helps provide a signal to LinkedIn about what you're genuinely interested in and if your Influencers have similar keywords to your list of primary and secondary keywords, that is a great bonus!

Don't forget that at the end of the list, there is a 'See More' option if what you are interested in is not listed at the beginning of the list. Once you have selected an Influencer, this person will be listed in the 'Influencers' Section underneath the 'Following' heading on your LinkedIn Profile.

Action 30: *View the Pulse Discover Link, view their suggestions and various Influencers and then select which Influencers you would like to follow in the future*

4.6 Select Your Channels (Following)

Once again, visit http://linkedin.com/pulse/discover to see a list of Channels that may be of interest to you. These channels are collections of articles and insights grouped by topic, so if you are specializing in a particular area, this is another great way to receive content aligned with your purpose (and to send the right signal to LinkedIn and Google).

Don't forget that at the end of the list, there is a 'See More' option if what you are interested in is not listed at the beginning of the list.

Once you have selected a Channel, this will be listed in the 'News' Section underneath the 'Following' heading on your LinkedIn Profile.

Action 31: *View the Pulse Discover Link, view their Channels list and then select which ones you would like to follow in the future*

4.7 Select Your News Publishers

Once again, visit http://linkedin.com/pulse/discover to see a list of News providers that may be of interest to you. These News profiles provide news from global and industry sources and these Publishers had to 'earn their stripes' before they were listed on LinkedIn. This is a great way to receive content aligned with your purpose (and to send the right signal once again) or just to keep you in the loop on current issues (because so many people have various specializations nowadays, unless a special effort is made, general news may not be seen).

Don't forget that at the end of the list, there is a 'See More' option if what you are interested in is not listed at the beginning of the list. Sometimes the Publishers listed further down are more relevant than the popular ones at the top. Once you have selected a Publisher, this will be listed in the 'News' Section of your LinkedIn Profile.

If receiving content is really important to you, consider downloading the LinkedIn Pulse App http://linkedin.com/mobile for your mobile device.

Action 32: *View the Pulse Discover Link, view their News Provider list and then select which ones you would like to follow in the future*

4.8 Decide How To Respond To Your News Feed

There is a saying in the social media world that you should spend 70% of your time sharing your own useful content, 20% of your time sharing other people's useful content and a maximum of 10% of your time sharing 'sales' content. I would argue that it is even better if you don't ever post a 'sales' message!

So as the news comes in to your News Feed – from your Connections, the Companies, Influencers and News Channels you follow, the Sponsored Ads, the Job Advertisements etc., you need to decide how you will respond.

The time you spend on this will depend on your purpose. That said, if you respond too often, again, you can appear desperate.

You must always, no matter how reliable the source, read the content in full before Liking, Commenting or Sharing.

If you do comment, please add some value (and don't shoot the messenger in the process). Saying 'Great update' gives no clues as to what was great. If you personalize it with the contributor's name (which will hyperlink when you type it), they will be notified that you have responded. If you include specifics about what was useful or informative, then it provides very useful feedback to the contributor and helps your own LinkedIn Profile if anyone else reads your comment.

Interacting with your news feed can be time consuming, particularly if you read the associated links. If the company or person providing the update is important for your purpose, it can be valuable and strengthen that relationship if you acknowledge their contribution with a Like, Comment and/or Share. You can acknowledge or notify people in your updates by typing '@' before you mention their name i.e. by typing '@Sue Ellson' you will see my name appear in a drop down box and you can select it.

If it is not closely related to your purpose, the 'lifetime value' of your interaction with the newsfeed is quite small – because it only appears in your newsfeed so unless someone sees your interaction at that time or visits your profile and looks at your 'Recent Activity,' they are unlikely to see your contribution (this is why I generally recommend writing and interacting with Posts which have a longer lifetime value).

Action 33: *Decide how and when you will Like, Comment and Share Updates that appear in your News Feed but remember to read the content in full before Liking, Commenting or Sharing*

4.9 Create A Schedule For Endorsing Skills Of Connections

You may have already added a list of Skills to your LinkedIn Profile and likewise, your Connections may have added Skills to their LinkedIn Profile. I encourage you to turn on the Settings in the Skills and Endorsements Section of your LinkedIn Profile so that you can be endorsed, included in endorsement suggestions to your connections, be shown suggestions to endorse your connections and receive notifications via email when your connections endorse you.

To do this, go to your LinkedIn Profile, scroll down to the Skills and Endorsements Section and click 'Add Skill' and tick the boxes and Save.

Some of my clients have become very concerned when they have received Endorsements from people they don't know or have never met. If you wish, you can 'Manage' your Endorsements and remove these unsolicited votes.

Personally, I choose not to worry about the extra endorsement votes. But I will never endorse another person unless I am very confident that they have the skills listed on their LinkedIn Profile and I have witnessed them directly.

LinkedIn's algorithms will reward some good behavior and I have found that if you start endorsing some of your Connections, LinkedIn may start mentioning your name to your Connections – so by voting for others, you may start to receive your own votes. I refer to this as 'feeding the beast.'

This is why I encourage you to periodically add a few Endorsements of Skills to your Connections Profiles. To do this, visit your Connection's LinkedIn Profile, scroll down to the Skills and

Endorsements Section and click the + next to the Skill where you would like to add your vote.

Alternatively, if you would like to do it a little more quickly, visit http://linkedin.com/profile/edit?showSuggestedEndorsements=true and then go through the suggestions LinkedIn provides.

Action 34: *Decide how and when you will accurately Endorse your Connections for their Skills*

4.10 Select A Recommendations Strategy

Writing Recommendations provides a range of benefits. It is a great way to publicly and permanently recognize a Connection's abilities. It can help strengthen a relationship (you took the time and effort to do it) and if their LinkedIn Profile includes similar keywords, it could be a great way to confirm your other keywords, activities and signals to the LinkedIn algorithms. It is also an excellent technique for sharing your LinkedIn Profile with a new audience – the people viewing your Connection's LinkedIn Profile!

But you need to be careful. It must never be seen as a way to manipulate the system and it is extremely important to only say what you are prepared to also say in court – yes, the details provided in Recommendations have previously been used as evidence in court.

If you feel obligated to write a reference and you do not feel comfortable about recommending the person for certain skills, focus on the skills that you are willing to recommend. For example, they may be a very difficult Project Manager with an autocratic management style, but they may have an excellent ability to accurately analyze complex data.

I am not a fan of using the LinkedIn 'ask for recommendations' tool at http://linkedin.com/recs/ask – I prefer to contact Connections personally and mention that I would like to write a recommendation for them but I would like to know what they would like me to focus on in my content first. If they choose to do so, they can, in turn, write a recommendation for me via http://linkedin.com/recs/give. Likewise, I give them some clues as to what I would like them to feature in the Recommendation they write for me. I always proof read their Recommendation before I publish it as I do not want them to be perceived incorrectly from a spelling or grammar mistake.

For example:

Dear Sandy,

Thank you for being a Connection of mine on LinkedIn. I would like to write a Recommendation for you on LinkedIn and after reviewing your LinkedIn Profile and based on my experience of working with you, I would like to highlight your excellent accounting, auditing and taxation skills.

Would these areas be the most appropriate items to highlight? If you would like me to mention other areas as well? Please let me know. Once I have sent the Recommendation through, you will need to approve it for publication on your LinkedIn Profile at http://linkedin.com/recs/received

Also, if you have a moment to write a Recommendation for me in return, I would really appreciate any feedback you can provide on my secretarial, administration and bookkeeping skills. To write a Recommendation, simply login to your LinkedIn account and visit http://linkedin.com/recs/give and type my name in the Search your Connections box and follow the prompts.

Thanks in advance for your help, and once again, please let me know if the items I have suggested are the most suitable to highlight in the recommendation that I write for you.

Yours sincerely,

Sharon Jones

You can also manage your Recommendations at http://linkedin.com/recs. If someone writes a Recommendation for you, before it appears on your LinkedIn Profile, you can request changes (particularly if there are technical errors).

When preparing a Recommendation, try and include some specific comments that help the reader understand the value your Connection provides. Think about what their keywords might be. Write in a concise and informative manner so that the reader can quickly decipher the results they may be able to expect from this person in the future. Try not to use descriptions like '27 years of experience' as this ages a person – talk about their specific skills, knowledge and networks.

Finally, you must be aware of any Social Media Policy Rules that you must abide by before you write a Recommendation on LinkedIn. In my first job, I was not allowed to write any form of reference on behalf of the organization where I worked.

Have a look at any Social Media Policy agreements you have signed to make sure that you are allowed to comment whilst you are in your current role (even though your Recommendation is essentially 'personal'). You may need to wait until you have left the organization to be able to write a Recommendation for a fellow employee.

Just as you would write three or more Posts a year, I encourage you to also write three or more Recommendations a year. You may also like to try and secure at least three new Recommendations from other people on your LinkedIn Profile each year. I also encourage you to try and secure one recommendation for each role you have had (even if it is not from a supervisor).

LinkedIn may also use the number of Recommendations you have as a way to determine whether your LinkedIn Profile should appear above someone else's in search results (I recommend you source at total of six recommendations on your own LinkedIn Profile). These written recommendations are also helpful if you are trying to secure work in another country in the future as they provide formal verifiable evidence of your past experience).

Action 35: *Write three or more concise and informative Recommendations for selected Connections each year*

4.11 Select A Connections Strategy

Deciding who you will connect with on LinkedIn is essentially a decision you will need to make based on your purpose.

In most cases, you will be making a conscious effort when you request a Connection (and it is always best if you personalize your request with an individual message by clicking the Connect button from the person's LinkedIn Profile rather than from the Connect button on the people you may know page at http://linkedin.com/people/pymk).

You can invite people to connect with you via email – and you can invite 10 people at a time and up to 100 a day by visiting http://

linkedin.com/fetch/importAndInviteEntry and choose 'Invite by email.' You can paste the email addresses in the box, separated by commas. Unfortunately, this only sends an 'I'd like to join your LinkedIn network' email and is not as likely to be accepted by the recipient.

You also have the option of adding your email address via this link. This will sync every contact in your email address book and add the contents of every email to the LinkedIn Platform. I am quite sure that most enterprises will not want you to do this with a work email address (especially for privacy reasons).

It has the 'advantage' of attaching all of your past and future email correspondence to that person in LinkedIn (if you are connected to them), but it also invites all of the contacts in your email program address book to LinkedIn and you may or may not want to automatically do this (for instance, you may have stopped communicating with some people and this process will trigger an automatic, non-personalized LinkedIn invitation Connection request).

In my view, the better option is to export all of your contacts from your email program address book and then personally invite the people you would like to connect to on LinkedIn directly via LinkedIn (not via syncing). You would do a search, visit their LinkedIn Profile, choose to Connect and write a brief introduction and send the invitation.

You may also like to connect with people in your profession or industry. If you are a member of a professional association, they sometimes list paid up members on their website and this could be a way for you to find and invite these people to your network on LinkedIn. It is a good way to build your profile in the sector and it is part of your professional network building that I discuss in Section 12.3.

If you send too many invitations and most of the people decline your Connection request, the LinkedIn algorithms will detect this behavior and reduce your ability to send further invitations – so be warned if you try to spam people, you will be caught!

Over the years, I have received a plethora of unwanted invitations from people who are spammers, unethical sales people who bombard me with sales emails and men of a certain age thinking that they can extort money from me by telling me how beautiful I am!

I have become quite mercenary when receiving these invitations and I no longer have any hesitation in declining these invitations and reporting them as spammers. If someone slips through and then sends me a sales message, I report the spam message and remove them as a Connection by visiting their LinkedIn Profile and clicking on the blue Drop Down Box and choosing 'Remove Connection.'

It is important for you to report spammers too – because LinkedIn does investigate these reports and regularly removes spammers from the LinkedIn Platform (thank goodness!).

Some people are quite pedantic when deciding whether or not to accept a Connection request on LinkedIn. They will often say that unless the invitation has been personalized, they will flatly refuse the request (regardless of who sent the invitation – even a close friend!).

Others, depending on which country or community they live in, will only connect with people they have met in person. Some people choose to only connect with people who share the exact same profession so that all of their connections, newsfeed, groups etc are exclusively related to the one topic.

Some people think that it is a good idea to have more than one LinkedIn Profile – one that is associated with one aspect of their lives and another one for a different component of their lives.

In my opinion, you are only one person and you should have only one LinkedIn Profile and use it to achieve multiple purposes (which can be done!). I do not recommend having duplicate profiles under any circumstances (see Section 2.1 to find out how to fix this issue). Even if you did go down this path, how would people know which LinkedIn Profile they should connect to?

Also, an email address can only be added to one LinkedIn Profile. So, if your new Connection sent an invitation to the wrong email address, you would have to ask them to Connect to the 'other' person instead. Too messy!

I do encourage you to add every old and every new email address you have to your LinkedIn Profile and never remove any old email addresses – because that way, people who have known you via a former email address can still 'find' you on LinkedIn.

This process will also prevent you receiving a new invitation to join LinkedIn with a different email address. I also recommend that you have your personal email address as your Primary LinkedIn Email Address, particularly if you are in job search mode because a recruiter will not want to email you in your current job.

The Social Media Policy of an enterprise may ask you to remove the enterprise email address from your LinkedIn Profile when you leave the enterprise, particularly if you have been in a management position. So if you have signed a Social Media Policy that makes this request, please remember to do it.

See Section 7.2 for more clues on how to assess a LinkedIn Profile and make a choice about whether or not you should accept a Connection invitation. I personally check every LinkedIn Profile before I say yes.

LinkedIn currently allows you to have up to 35,000 LinkedIn Connections on your account.

Having more Connections (rather than less Connections), will increase your search results (more first and second level Connections will come up in your searches), but remember, these Connections are also part of the Signals you are sending to LinkedIn.

The bottom line is this – you can decide who to connect to on LinkedIn (or who to remove), based on your purpose. Remember that the more people who have the same keywords as you in their LinkedIn Profile, the more 'relevant' your LinkedIn Profile will be in search results for those keywords.

Having more Connections than someone else is not necessarily the goal here. What you are trying to do is achieve your purpose – so select a strategy that works to achieve that (if you want a ballpark number of Connections to increase by each year, I would say by about 5-10% just to keep yourself active in the market). The most relevant people could possibly be in the Groups that you have joined and participate in frequently.

Finally, as I have a variety of enterprises and a lot of people are leaving email lists nowadays as they want to reduce the number of emails they receive, I have developed a policy of personally inviting the people who have unsubscribed from my mailing lists to connect with me on LinkedIn – and interestingly, up to 50% of these invitations have been accepted! That means that I can still keep in touch with these people through LinkedIn – even though they are no longer part of my email newsletter list.

Action 36: *Select a Connection Strategy based on your purpose, remembering that Connections with similar keywords will help you appear in LinkedIn Search Results*

4.12 Decide What You Will Do On A Regular Basis

As always, what you decide to do on a regular basis will depend on your purpose – but in this section, I will provide a range of options for you to consider.

To make sure you take action, you may need to set up your own schedule and add it to your diary or calendar.

- **Maintenance** (three monthly) – record your number of views to your LinkedIn Profile for the last 90 days (and your Company or Group Statistics if relevant). Complete any updates to your LinkedIn Profile and save a copy of your LinkedIn Profile to a PDF document. Export your Connections and save it as a Microsoft Outlook CSV file on your computer or the cloud. Collect any other statistics you deem to be relevant (see Section 2.6)

- **Updates to your LinkedIn Profile** (three monthly) – review what sections you can have on your LinkedIn Profile (as new options may have been added) and also add in any new information (new job, certification, education or training completed etc)

- **Every time you login to LinkedIn** – respond to messages you have received, have a quick glance over your notifications (and respond to any comments on your Posts or Updates) and review the Connection requests and decide whether or not to accept them or not

If you have time, consider reviewing some items in your personal newsfeed http://linkedin.com/home, your company newsfeed http://linkedin.com/company/home and group discussions http://linkedin.com/groups (and Like, Comment or Share provided you have reviewed any links and comments in full first)

- **Follow Up** – if you have chosen to create a list of VIP contacts or you have set some reminders within LinkedIn, spend a few moments connecting with these people on a personal basis, particularly if they are good referral sources for now or the future

- **Thank You's** – you may like to take a few moments to thank someone for connecting with you, endorsing you for skills or for writing a recommendation. You could include a "thanks for sharing" comment in either an Update or a Post in Pulse (but also mention what was so informative)

- **Good Behavior** – send some good Signals to LinkedIn. Where relevant (and appropriate based on evidence), endorse some people for a selection of the skills on their LinkedIn Profile and write a suitable recommendation for one or more of your Connections.

  Consider personally inviting a few people you know to connect with you on LinkedIn (assuming they are not already connected to you!) and reach out to a few new people that are related to your purpose via the People You May Know feature http://linkedin.com/people/pymk. Review some job advertisements http://linkedin.com/job/home if you could be in the job market within the next 12 months

- **Reverse Stalking** – by having a look at the people who have been looking at your LinkedIn Profile http://linkedin.com/wvmx/profile you can determine whether or not your LinkedIn Profile is attracting the right audience for your purpose. You may also choose to personally contact some of these people. If you are not attracting the right audience or response, consider changing your content

- **Ethical Stalking** – consider having a look at a few LinkedIn Profiles (or Companies or Groups) on LinkedIn for general research or industry updates. If required, you can change your settings to Private Mode before looking at a person's LinkedIn Profile via your Privacy and Settings Menu on the top right hand side of your screen https://linkedin.com/settings/summary by adjusting the 'Select what others see when you've viewed their profile' to the third option – Private Mode. Turn it back to the Name and Headline Mode when you have finished. I do not recommend this activity for repeated viewing of one person's profile but it could be very appropriate for due diligence, interview preparation, financial loan assessments, recruitment head hunting etc. and as a cold calling technique (see Section 5.2)

- **Reach out to someone for a personal catch up** – it could be a direct SMS, a phone call or a face to face meeting – just remember that you can't network exclusively online – some of the most successful opportunities are created in person. If you instigate a meeting with someone, I encourage you to pay for any refreshments and if the other person offers to pay, politely suggest that they can pay the next time you meet. If you agree to meet for a certain time period, make sure that you give the person an option to leave at the agreed time point before continuing your discussion

- **Understand that there are different processes for different purposes** – for example, as a job seeker, you are likely to focus on different regular activities than you would as a private consultant or CEO of a major corporation. Some of these suggestions can be outsourced to a trusted consultancy, in-house communications team or a virtual assistant but others need to be done by you and you alone.

Action 37: *Choose what actions you will do on a regular basis to achieve your purpose with LinkedIn*

5. Job Search Strategies

As mentioned earlier, up to 90% of jobs are no longer advertised. The jobs that are available and the way that they are found is constantly changing. Some people have suggested that the world is moving towards a 'Gig Economy' where no-one will have full time jobs, each person will just complete a range of 'gigs' (artists and musicians have been doing this for years). But we are also in the 'Knowledge Age' – an environment where we need to inspire and educate in an environment that is full of clutter.

Whether you are looking for full time, part time, casual, temporary or contract work, in this section, I will showcase a range of Job Search Strategies you can utilize to attract the right opportunity that matches your purpose.

There is some interesting information around about intrinsic motivation in terms of employment. If you seek work based on your purpose and you believe that the role will be both fulfilling and inspirational, you are up to 10 times more likely to stay with the enterprise.

If your motivation is based on people and the level of engagement and perks you receive, you are six times more likely to stay with the enterprise.

Finally, if your motivation is based on profit and the opportunity for professional development or just to get a job, you are least likely to stay with the enterprise.

I hope this helps you to pause and realize that you are far better off attracting a job that will be fulfilling and inspirational to you. You may wish to think about how much autonomy you would like, how many skills you would like to use or develop and how much you would like to relate to other people to narrow down your focus.

Action 38: *Understand that most jobs are no longer advertised and you will need to attract the right opportunities in the future*

5.1 Select A Range Of Concurrent Strategies

LinkedIn is a key component of many job search strategies for a variety of reasons:

- it gives employers access to passive talent (people who will move for the right opportunity)

- it enables employers to verify information they hear about via a referral (if you Google someone's name, and they have a LinkedIn Profile, it is likely to appear on the first page of Google Search Results)

- it is a source of job advertisements

- it is a way for people to search their existing networks to find someone suitable to refer to their current employer

- it can offer job seekers a way to find out information about their potential employer and the staff who work there

- it can help you find companies that may have roles that will suit you

A personal Job Search Strategy should include a range of concurrent strategies. It is never a good idea to rely on one technique alone. Some of my most successful clients have had up to 10 different processes running at the same time to find the right opportunity for the next stage of their career. They have also been willing to say 'no' if the 'wrong' opportunity appears.

Action 39: *Select a variety of LinkedIn and Other Job Search Strategies if you are looking for work and utilize all of them until you find the right opportunity aligned with your purpose*

5.2 Do Your Research

You can complete a variety of Advanced Searches on LinkedIn (even with the free account) to find suitable individuals to contact and Companies to Follow.

Did you know that if you visit a person's LinkedIn Profile, there is up to a 30% chance that they will look at your LinkedIn Profile? This is an excellent Cold Calling technique that has the potential to spark some interest in your value offering – particularly if that value is clearly demonstrated via your Photo, Headline and Summary sections

---

Also, as mentioned in Section 4.3, if you are already Following a Company where you would like to work, you have a greater chance of coming up in their LinkedIn Search Results if they are using LinkedIn Recruitment Tools.

You will often see a box on your screen that says 'People You May Know,' 'People Also Viewed,' 'People Similar,' 'Ads You May Be Interested In' and 'Jobs You May Be Interested In.' These boxes can lead you to useful content that may be helpful for your Job Search.

When you look at Company Profiles, there could be a Careers Section and it can include How You Are Connected to the Company, Jobs currently available, Featured Employees, Recent Updates, a comprehensive company description and links to further information. This information should be compulsory reading before applying for a job and attending an interview.

Action 40: *Use the Advanced Search Tool to find a variety of information about Individuals and Companies you may like to work with in the future*

5.3 Find Suitable Mentors Through LinkedIn

I have often worked with clients to source suitable Job Search Mentors. You need to find people who have a common range of interests, values or purposes. This is best explained by example.

I was working with a professional architect from overseas who had moved to Melbourne. At the time of his arrival, the industry was in a downturn phase as very few projects could gather funding for development. Together we completed some searches on LinkedIn and we found a person who was particularly well connected in the industry.

This person had international experience, they were an adviser to various professional associations and also listed a variety of voluntary positions on their LinkedIn Profile. My client telephoned this person to find out more information about the industry in Melbourne and whilst this person did not have any current opportunities available, he offered to meet my client and discuss a variety of options for the future.

When sourcing a Job Search Mentor, it is important to approach the person in a professional manner and only ask for information in the first stage. If they appear to be interested in helping you, I recommend that you suggest that they be your Job Search Mentor. This would involve an in-person meeting and then occasional emails and phone calls over a period of three months. Any refreshments that are consumed during this time should be paid for by you. When you invite them to be your mentor, they have the option of saying either 'yes' or 'no' – and if they say no, you simply move on and look for someone else.

This Job Search Mentor does not necessarily need to be in exactly the same industry or profession. They may have a similar country of origin or they may be in another location but have worked in your current location (for example, they may now be in Thailand but were previously in Melbourne and you are looking for work in Melbourne). You simply need to 'select' the right Job Search Mentor just as you need to 'match' yourself with the right job or referrers.

"I always wish I'd had more mentors, better mentors, wiser mentors, people who were proper professional working musicians to guide me as I was coming up." Keith Urban

Action 41: *Utilize LinkedIn to select a Job Search Mentor to help match you with the right job or referrers*

5.4 Reach Out To Your Network

When was the last time you reached out to your Connections on LinkedIn to let them know what your purpose is on LinkedIn? A personalized message to selected Connections can be a great way to start conversations that can lead to opportunities. It is important to be as descriptive as possible – for example:

Dear Rick,

Thank you for being a Connection of mine here on LinkedIn. I have been working in my current Project Management role for the last two years and have now been working with XYZ Organization for the last five years.

I have just finished updating my LinkedIn Profile to include the details of some of the Projects I have recently completed.

I am now starting to look for new roles in the area of Senior Project Management in other organizations in either Engineering or Manufacturing in Sydney.

I would welcome confidential suggestions you might have or referrals to people who may be able to provide more information.

Likewise, if I can assist you in any way, I would be more than happy to help you.

I look forward to hearing from you soon Rick.

Yours sincerely,

Sue Ellson

+61 402 222 333

sueellson@sueellson.com

http://au.linkedin.com/in/sueellson

These messages are even better if you spend a few moments reviewing Rick's LinkedIn Profile and include a personal comment about his LinkedIn Profile or your past correspondence.

Action 42: *Contact individual Connections on LinkedIn and ask for suggestions or referrals to help lead you to your next opportunity*

5.5 Apply For Jobs Listed On LinkedIn

Visit the Jobs Page at http://linkedin.com/job/home and conduct a search for the jobs that match your purpose. The advertised positions will allow you to either 'Apply via The Company Website' or 'Apply through LinkedIn.' If you apply through LinkedIn, you have an opportunity to either send through a link to your LinkedIn Profile or send your link and Upload a File (they suggest a Resume / Cover Letter).

As you can only upload one file, I suggest that you create an 'Application' Document which has a cover letter on the first page and a resume on the following pages. You absolutely must tailor this application for the job advertised, incorporating specific responses to their requirements. Standard click through applications that just link to your LinkedIn Profile are unlikely to secure an interview or further interest.

Your LinkedIn Profile is the 'full story' of your background. The Job Application is the 'part of the story' that is related to the job description.

Save the decision maker the trouble of matching the advertisement with your application by doing the work for them and showcasing the most relevant items in your cover letter and resume. You will have a much better chance of securing a job interview because your application will 'match' their job description (or advertisement).

If you are applying for a job from a remote location, please include how you plan to work in the new location in the future (and how you will secure the necessary work rights or visa).

I would also like to share a quick example about the importance of standing out in a pile of job applicants. When I have been in a recruitment role and scanning through multiple applications, I have found it very easy to forget the details of individual candidates, particularly if their application is very comprehensive but boring.

One of my clients was applying for a role as a tour guide for a very well-known local art gallery. This is a very prestigious role in the local arts community and the quality of applicants and the level of competition for these roles is extremely high. One of the questions that needed to be answered in the 'Key Selection Criteria' for this position was "Do you speak any other languages?" She only spoke English but she could also lip read. Naturally you can imagine that if an applicant could speak multiple languages in this role, it would be very helpful.

Now as you already know, lip reading is not an actual 'language' as such, but for this role, it was a perfect skill to highlight in this section of her application. It would be very useful as a tour guide to be able to lip read people in a noisy environment or with a disparate group, so this detail made her application extremely memorable (where is that applicant who can lip read?) and finally, it shows a bit of creative flair when answering the question. She got the job.

Action 43: *Always include a tailored 'Application' document with any job you apply for through LinkedIn*

5.6 View The Career Sections Of Selected Companies

Employers do not always advertise every job they have available on LinkedIn or any other website. Some employers even create jobs for 'talent' that they find. By looking at Company Pages on LinkedIn, you can find out whether the Company also advertises jobs on their Company Website and then follow the instructions to register your interest directly. My first employer never advertised at all because they always had enough people who contacted them directly to register their interest.

If you are going to use this technique, make sure that you update your Personal Profile on the Company's Career Section of their website at least every three months. This is the 'average' length of time your profile is accessed before it is archived as employers make the assumption that you would 'find' work within three months and no longer be in the market for an opportunity.

Action 44: *View the Career Section of Company Pages to research jobs through the Company website*

5.7 Connect With Recruiters

As you review job advertisements on LinkedIn related to your purpose, you are likely to find that a range of jobs advertised in a particular industry or profession are with the same Recruitment Company. It is therefore a good idea to view the Company Page for these recruiters and also find out if you are connected to anyone who can introduce you to the Recruiters who work there. A direct referral from someone they already know is much more likely to be successful than if you try and contact them directly.

Likewise, I encourage you to connect with recruiters who have been in their role for more than five years. These recruiters are more likely to be receptive to good quality candidates because they understand that to be successful in recruitment, you need to have a network of passive and active candidates on standby. Use LinkedIn to view their recruitment history and choose the most appropriate way to reach out to them.

Action 45: *Visit Recruiter Company Pages to find recruiters who can help you achieve your purpose*

5.8 Connect With Professional Association Members

I highly recommend that you join a professional association related to your profession or industry. You can then showcase your Membership on your LinkedIn Profile in the Certifications and Organizations Sections as well as include your Post Nominals in your Summary Section. You may also wish to link to the Association in your Website Links part of your Contact Info Section.

The main benefit of becoming a professional association member is that you gain access to a network of like-minded individuals. These people, as fellow members, are more likely to provide information that may be helpful to you. If they hold an official role, they are also likely to be well informed and well connected.

They may be able to suggest that you attend certain events or forums, that you participate in a mentoring or certification program or that you get involved in a voluntary capacity so that you can network with people of influence directly.

If they share other commonalities with you, they may be willing to provide you with a referral. This is still one of the most successful ways to secure work or business. Remember though that you must always personally say 'thank you' for any assistance or referrals you receive.

Action 46: *After joining a professional association, maximize your online brand and connect directly with other association members to achieve your purpose*

5.9 Tailor Your Photo, Headline And Summary

The three main sections that people view when they look at your LinkedIn Profile are the Photo, Headline and Summary. As up to 70% of humans are more visual than auditory or kinesthetic, the photo is vital. Most viewers will spend up to 20% of their time looking at your photo when they view your LinkedIn Profile – they will spend even more time if it is a bad photo (which is a bad thing because you don't want them to just look at your photo, you want them to read your LinkedIn Profile).

Your LinkedIn Profile Photo must be aligned with your purpose. (A quick tip, put some light makeup face powder on your skin so that your skin doesn't appear shiny in the photo and if you are worried about a double chin look, put your chin forward and then your face downwards before taking the photo).

Your Headline provides the quick snapshot of your value offering so it is also vitally important (and your primary keywords in this location can generate search results).

You do not want to mention that you are 'seeking opportunities' in your headline – this makes you look desperate and does not have any keyword search value.

Your Summary also needs to be aligned with your purpose. If you are passively or actively seeking work, you can write your Summary accordingly. You can make it clear what sort of opportunities you are interested in and provide your contact details so that decision makers can contact you directly (without waiting until they are connected to you or paying for a Premium membership http://linkedin.com/premium/products to send you an InMail).

You can also word this in a way that does not arouse suspicion with your current employer. For example, you can say you 'specialize in' and include your contact details and viewers then know that they can reach out to you. If you are actively seeking work, you can say 'interested in roles in' instead.

If your past is in a different area, it is still okay to provide these details. This will mean that your Photo, Headline and Summary will need to really showcase your new purpose and be focused on your new direction and you need to think about using keywords that apply from both your previous career and your new career.

You may not know that your Photo, Headline and Summary are usually visible to the public in a Google Search Result (unless you have turned them to private) even if the person is not signed in to LinkedIn at that moment. This is why it is important to include your most important content in these three sections.

Action 47: *Ensure that your Photo, Headline and Summary are perfectly aligned with your purpose*

5.10 Understand Job Search Algorithms

If you apply for jobs online and submit a resume, there is a strong possibility that your details will be added to an Applicant Tracking System (ATS) – a database where all of the job applicant resumes are kept. Over time, these systems have become extremely good at sifting through applications and producing a short list of applicants. If you do not understand how these work, you can be eliminated from the first round of processing.

So you need to think about the decision maker and what they will be seeking. You must NEVER EVER lie on LinkedIn or your resume, but if there are primary and secondary keywords that you believe are likely to be in a search query selected by a decision maker, then you need to make every effort to include these in as many of your past roles as possible.

This has the advantage of 'proving' that you have XX years of experience. If you only write this keyword in your current job, your years of experience will only be taken from your current role.

If you also incorporate these keywords in other locations – your headline, summary, education, skills, projects, certifications, organizations, publications etc., this will also help. If you then incorporate the keywords in your signals – posts, updates, messages, activity, endorsements, recommendations, connections etc., you have an even greater chance.

LinkedIn does not allow fancy formatting in each of the boxes where you enter information (but as stated earlier, please add in website links as these will be clickable on mobile devices).

Unfortunately, when you create a resume, you can add in various fonts, tables, headings, text boxes, images and other formatting which is not recognized in Applicant Tracking Systems and basically renders a large proportion of your content invalid. So remember to only have bold and plain text in your resume – which should also be a Word

Document rather than a PDF so that if any formatting is required by the recruiter, it will be quick and easy to do.

Action 48: *Optimize your LinkedIn content by ensuring your primary and secondary keywords are mentioned in multiple sections of your LinkedIn Profile and in your LinkedIn Signals*

5.11 Prepare For Job Interviews

Whilst you will want your LinkedIn Profile and your resume to come up in search results, ultimately it is not just a computer that will be 'reading' your content. A real person will be reading your content. If you have worked exclusively on maximizing keywords and your content doesn't make any logical sense, you will not get past the second round of processing. You will not be able to convince the reader to contact you.

If you do get past the second round of processing and you are fortunate to be selected for an interview, you can make the assumption that your skills are adequate for the role. If you ask for feedback after the interview, particularly if you were not successful, and you are advised that you did not have enough experience, remember that this is a 'safe' answer from an employer.

Let me explain why. Most decision makers believe that they are using fair and equitable recruitment processes based on your skills, knowledge and networks, but they often fall into the trap of assessing how well you will fit into the current culture of the organization and the main reason you are actually not successful after an interview is because they could not see you fitting in at the organization.

As a job seeker, you need to have the confidence to realize that if you are unsuccessful, it was their loss and perhaps they were not the right fit for you. If you approach job seeking in this way – it has to be the right fit both ways – you will have a much greater chance of success – because you will not be desperate.

Let me give you an example. When I first moved to Melbourne, it only took me six weeks to find a job. I had five separate interviews and every time, I was told that I had come 'second.' I was extremely frustrated as I believed that this was the same as coming 'last' – I still did not have a job.

The next interview I went to, I started asking questions about the organization – how long people had worked there, what sort of history they had etc. I told them that I had a very successful career in Adelaide and I wanted to make sure I was heading in the right career direction in my new location. They offered me three different jobs – in the first interview! I was polite (not boastful), but I wanted to make it clear it had to be a good fit in both directions (a bit of reverse psychology where they had to 'get' me before someone else did!).

Before your job interview, you can use LinkedIn to do some research on the enterprise and perhaps even the people who will be interviewing you. If you prefer, you can look at their LinkedIn Profiles anonymously by going into your LinkedIn Settings http://linkedin.com/settings and changing the setting for 'Select what others see when you've viewed their profile' and change it to the third option of 'Private Mode.'

Once you have finished viewing their information, go back to your Settings and change it to the top option so that you can continue to see your LinkedIn Profile statistics and who has visited your profile (I call this reverse stalking – and when I look at who has looked at my LinkedIn Profile, it helps me determine whether or not my LinkedIn Profile is working for my purpose – and it is also a good way to start prospecting).

Action 49: *Utilize LinkedIn to do some background research on individuals and enterprises before your job interviews*

5.12 The Key To Job Search Success

The most successful job search strategy can be summed up in one word, persistence.

If you need to make phone calls, visit organizations, apply for jobs online, attend networking events, have a Job Search Mentor, source referrals, complete voluntary work or a job placement, attend a workshop or course, schedule information gathering interviews, approach companies directly, work with recruiters, participate in an outplacement program, seek assistance from a career development practitioner, work with a career coach or adviser or do all of these, the person who keeps on persisting with multiple concurrent strategies will eventually be successful.

As a good example of persistence, when my son was 13, he was under age for working in Australia and he did not have a resume – but he wanted to work in aged care. He simply telephoned aged care facilities until someone said yes. When he wanted more work, he started making more telephone calls once again. He didn't stop when someone said no. He kept going. Persistence.

The essential component of any strategy is to be clear on your purpose! Once you are clear on this, you can select the best strategies that will move you closer to that purpose.

If you are not clear, secure some professional advice from a trusted expert or Career Development Practitioner – why waste your time going in the wrong direction? Once you receive this advice, test it before moving forward. Securing some real life experience will help you confirm your selection.

Once you are clear on your purpose, you need to select the most effective strategies for your purpose. The person who utilizes more than one job search technique has an even greater chance of success.

For example, if you want to work in some industries, the main way you can secure work is via a direct referral by someone who knows you in the industry. This would obviously be one of your top priority strategies. You still would not use this technique exclusively.

You may also like to reach out to people who have looked at your LinkedIn Profile. If you are going to do this, pay it forward by offering them a link to something useful for their purpose, some premium content in a white paper or eBook that you send via email or perhaps even a suggestion to connect to someone you know. This is likely to be appreciated far more than 'please give me a job.'

Once again, remember that the skills to find a job are different to the skills to do a job.

If you are in a position where you need to find a 'job to pay the bills right now,' then you may be a little bit more flexible on the type of job you would like to find. This can still be viewed as a step towards your longer term goal.

My only warning here is, please do not plateau. Do not get comfortable with a certain income and give up on your dreams – it is never too late – with the right strategy over a reasonable time frame, you can aim for an 80%+ alignment with your purpose.

You also need to be realistic. If you have a range of personal commitments – like caring for children or family members, limited financial resources or skills or a health issue that needs additional support, you will need to make some choices based on your highest values as well as local market conditions.

For example, one of my highest values has been to spend time with my children – but I am also extremely intellectual and need to spend time doing work that challenges me. When my children were in primary school, after school care finished at 6pm and if I was going to have a full time job, I needed to be at the school by 6pm to collect them, without fail.

Unfortunately, most of the jobs aligned with my abilities were too far away for me to be able to return to the after school care by 6pm. So I chose to do a range of other activities to keep my mind active (part time study, voluntary work and my own business consulting), so that I could still achieve my highest value, spending time with my children. I did not 'lose' any value from my career because I also kept my skills and networks current. My overall job search strategy matched my purpose.

Action 50: *Be persistent with multiple concurrent strategies to achieve your purpose*

6. Career Development

I believe that Career Development involves helping you come to well considered decisions based on your strengths and preferences using a process that works for you. I also believe that this process can be enhanced by consulting a professional in practice – someone who has a good quality toolkit of resources to help you make these choices, is not biased for any reason and can support you throughout the process of achieving your goals.

If you are a professional career adviser, I encourage you to utilize the LinkedIn Platform as a vehicle for career counselling. Helping your client collect and compile the information required for a well completed LinkedIn Profile can be a great catalyst for a healthy discussion about future options and give you an opportunity to review what has worked well or not so well in the past, identify strengths and move forward in constructive ways.

Action 51: *To clarify your purpose and stay on track with what suits you both personally and professionally, please consider sourcing some expert assistance from a non-biased career development practitioner (or follow all of the recommendations in this book so that you can come to these conclusions yourself)*

6.1 Identifying Choices And Making Decisions

To determine your purpose, I like asking questions – and it starts with identifying your non-negotiables. This gives us a starting point to work with.

It also involves looking at all of the essential elements in your life, learning (study) and work. It incorporates understanding your family and cultural background, your experiences to date, your strengths and weaknesses and challenging any assumptions that you may have that are limiting your potential. I like to do this in a calm, confidential and supportive manner.

It also involves creating a framework for you to explore a wide range of possibilities and make productive and realistic choices based on your personal circumstances, study, career, labor market conditions and local environment.

*It also involves you taking some responsibility for doing some further research –
both direct information gathering and asking questions of various people.*

It can involve looking at both the long and short term beliefs you have and perhaps revising some of these and really questioning whether they still apply right now. You may have always thought you wanted to do something, but when you look a little closer, you may actually realize that you are happy with most of what is happening in your life right now! Try not to lock yourself into any absolutes.

Some Career Development Practitioners use skills or personality assessment tools to help you with this process. I see these as complementary to the process and the practitioner must be suitably qualified to use these tools (and constructive and supportive during the debriefing process). I also see this as only part of the process – I would never recommend that you rely on a tool to make a decision for you.

Ultimately, the final decision around your purpose, now and in the future, is always YOURS – not someone else's. You are the one who must make the ultimate choices about your life, based on your values. You may like to complete the 'Life Area Values and Purpose Table' mentioned in Section 1.3 if you haven't already done so.

Try not to rush your decision making process if you are still unsure about your purpose or what you want to do next. Keep collecting the information you need and if necessary, discuss your options with someone who does not have a vested interest in any particular outcome.

Sometimes verbalizing your concerns and options can help you come to a conclusion. A good listener can sometimes be just as helpful as a good adviser, especially if they reflect your comments back to you and seek further clarification.

I personally have difficulty reaching decisions for complex personal situations. It often annoys me too – because I would really appreciate finishing the process of coming to a successful decision quickly! But that's the point. I like to make successful decisions, not just any

Sue Ellson

decision – so remember, as you go through the various processes mentioned in this book, or seek assistance from a career development professional, the final decisions are always yours and you need to be happy with your choices.

I have found that setting a 'due date' for my complex decisions helps. I have to answer all of my questions and concerns before that moment in time and really understand what it is I need to collect to make my decision. I don't always make the final decision on that particular date, but I usually do so within a few days of the due date.

What I can assure you is that when I do make my final decision, I don't have any regrets – because I have weighed up all of my options beforehand. I also decide that I will live with any consequences that occur, because I absolutely did my best when I made my well informed decision.

You need to understand how you make your decisions (and it could be different to mine!) and how you will respond if the consequences don't go according to plan.

No decision is ever a complete disaster – you will always learn something and sometimes, it is perfectly okay to make a decision that is 'good for now' and make your next decision a little later.

For example, you may wish to explore a particular work choice in one location but if you find out that the options are extremely limited, you could identify other options and put in place additional strategies for future success. You may start off with a job that pays the bills until you find a job that matches your career aspirations.

LinkedIn can help you find people who may be able to help you with the information gathering process.

LinkedIn could help you locate people in the profession or industry you are considering. It could lead to discussions with reputable advisers or consultants. It could connect you with subject matter experts or thought leaders.

LinkedIn has a huge range of Posts in Pulse http://linkedin.com/pulse. If you would like to search for Posts on your area of interest, use the Search Box on the top of your screen when you are logged into LinkedIn and on the left hand side of that box, click on the drop down list and choose 'Posts' so that you can search by keywords in Posts – then pick what you would like to read and even contact the author if it is particularly useful.

LinkedIn Company Pages can give you further insights. Reputable Professional Associations usually have a moderated LinkedIn Group that can give you further information. You may even like to view a few SlideShare Presentations http://slideshare.net

All of these sources can lead to additional websites and information portals – so make sure you keep a record of the best details so that you can follow up again later if you would like to investigate something more thoroughly. A spreadsheet or database of links is usually more helpful than a table list in a Word document – because you can sort the links!

Action 52: *Find information via people, posts and pages on LinkedIn to help make decisions related to your purpose*

6.2 Understanding The Local Market

Various locations around the world have excellent sources of information about the local labor or enterprise market. Unfortunately, quantitative data can sometimes be out of date, not specific enough for your purpose or simply unavailable to the public. Qualitative data, provided it is not used on an anecdotal basis for important decisions, can provide unique insights and sometimes, generate opportunities.

As you probably already know, the labor and enterprise market is constantly changing. What was popular and well paid in the past may now be scarce, superseded and/or low paid. The rate of change is so rapid that usually, within five to seven years, a role can be completely transformed – so now it is extremely important to keep your skills up to date through continuous learning and your networks alive through regular contact.

Your networks can also provide financial security. I usually state that there is 'no such thing as job security in any location.' However, you can create financial security and ongoing employability by building and maintaining a good network – and LinkedIn is a networking tool! (No, they didn't pay me to say that!!).

As Porter Gale says, "Your network is your net-worth."

Investing in relationships is also a way to invest in your retirement (and good relationships also make your life right now a lot more fun!)

So if you want to find out information about a local market, you need to complete adequate research based on both quantitative and qualitative data and determine what options are available both now and in the future.

Maintaining your employability is also vital (by keeping your skills, knowledge and networks up to date).

You can understand and identify trends and prepare for the future by undertaking further training, on the job experience, professional development, coaching or mentoring.

You also need to learn the various ways to access the local job or enterprise market because this can also change (so you need to use a range of strategies to be successful). For example, in the past, information about job vacancies was available via advertisements in newspapers – and now, there are hardly any jobs at all advertised in newspapers (except local or regional newspapers).

LinkedIn can keep you in the loop with local markets and trends through your Newsfeed, your participation in Groups and updates shared by the Companies you are following. Keeping in regular contact with your Connections, professional peers, key thought leaders and subject matter experts can also be helpful.

Try not to be too disillusioned if the level of demand has decreased dramatically in your area of expertise. I have worked with a broadcast engineer from Columbia and we found out via local quantitative data that most of the people in these roles in Australia were educated at Certificate level rather than Degree Level and that the current demand for these roles was quite low.

We checked LinkedIn and found that there were very few potential candidates on LinkedIn so we made the executive decision to pursue this career as well as one other career stream as she still has a chance of securing a role in broadcasting if her LinkedIn Profile comes up first in LinkedIn Search Results.

Action 53: *Source local job or enterprise market information via your Newsfeed, Group Discussions, and Company Updates and maintain contact with people in your networks*

6.3 Overcoming Barriers To Entry

After working with a variety of clients over many years, I have often found that it is not the local market that is a barrier to employment or enterprise. It could be one or several of the following perceived barriers:

- a lack of confidence or belief in your ability or value

- the influence of your partner, children, friends, parents or colleagues

- the assumptions you have made about the local market

- the various anecdotes you have heard that you have turned into beliefs

- a belief that your personal circumstances are preventing you from taking the next step (there could be alternatives)

- a sense of overwhelm (possibly as a result of anxiety or depression)

- procrastination (particularly if you are trying to achieve perfection with the first step)

- unrealistic expectations (particularly if you have had a very high salary in the past)

- past disappointments that remain unresolved or are still causing grief (either personally or professionally)

- the comments that you choose to remember and replay in your own mind that are not helpful

When I ask clients particular questions, I often uncover these possible barriers and then we explore them in more detail. Let me share an example.

I had a client who was working for a business that was exploiting her skills, underpaying her and the workplace was actually unsafe. She had come from another country where she had established a very successful dance school and she had excellent IT skills.

Unfortunately, despite her past successes, she did not feel that she was successful because her family of origin believed that you are only successful if you secure work as a doctor or a lawyer. In her mind, she believed she would never be successful unless she was a doctor or a lawyer.

Once we discovered this false belief, we explored what she was really interested in. Because she was unable to have children, she wanted to complete further studies and work in childcare. After quitting her job and travelling with her husband overseas for a year (a huge first step I might add), she completed childcare studies and secured the work she wanted.

She was very successful in this role – and then realized she would prefer to teach childcare workers – so she came to see me again. She changed jobs again. She is now living according to her values and as her purpose continues to change over time, she adjusts. I always like receiving updates from this client, because she continues to live her life with true purpose and meaning and she always seems to be smiling.

Once you understand the personal barriers you may have, you can re-evaluate the information you have collected and decide whether or not you need more information before you make your next decision and decide what action you will take. As Ronald Reagan has said, "There are no constraints on the human mind, no walls around the human spirit, no barriers to our progress except those we ourselves erect."

If you seek further personal assistance at this point, look for someone who has resolved all of their own issues and biases and can help you explore the best options for your needs and wants.

Make sure that any advisor you work with also understands the local market conditions and the additional learning, time or finance required (and are not biased in any way).

I do not believe it is a good idea to make a wholesale change and quit one thing and immediately start something else, especially on a whim. I encourage you to consider some transitional concepts. Perhaps you can investigate some other options through voluntary work, part time activities or work experience.

There is no need to 'throw the baby out with the bath water' and start from scratch when you are not happy with your present circumstances – regardless of your background, you will always have some transferable skills and something new to learn. You may just need to work for a different organization rather than a different profession.

It may also be necessary to consult a qualified counselor, health or wellbeing professional. After being sacked when I was pregnant, whenever I thought about that moment, I would become bitter and angry, and it lasted for six and a half years! I finally took action and read a book about forgiveness. I took their advice and resolved the issue. If I had taken that action earlier, I could have avoided all of that grief!

You may also wish to find a suitable mentor or coach to keep you on track and moving forward once you have made your career or enterprise choices. Remember, don't just talk about it, take action. If you need help, ask for it.

I have found that one of the most productive ways to overcome these possible barriers is to encourage you to fully complete your LinkedIn Profile, to the best of your ability. Past clients have often told me how it has brought back a lot of good memories about what they have achieved in the past.

But the second stage is even more exciting. When I review what they have written, I often find that it only tells part of the story. I ask them more questions and discover that their achievements were actually far more significant and definitely worth sharing.

I help them write out these achievements in a professional manner and sometimes, they have ended up in tears – of happiness – because someone has recognized their value and contribution (paid or unpaid).

It is never too late to move towards your purpose. Please don't let any past barriers stop you from moving forward in the future!

Sue Ellson

Action 54: *Identify your own barriers to success and complete as much of your LinkedIn Profile as possible*

6.4 Massaging The Message

There have been times when I have had to help people 'massage the message' that is shared on LinkedIn. I will categorically state that under no circumstances, will I ever encourage anyone to lie.

Some people have had a difficult past. Times when they have been unwell, unlawful, unproductive or unsuccessful, for whatever reason. This does not have to hold anyone back from a positive future.

Let's explore some ways that you or someone you know can overcome past challenges:

- **include any voluntary work you have done in the Experience section** – but don't mention it is voluntary – this is particularly useful if the voluntary work is related to your purpose and you can still include it in the Voluntary section as well (I have done this for my work with a Professional Association – the Australian Human Resources Institute – because it is aligned with my professional skills, but my voluntary work in catering and sailing with scouts is only included in the Voluntary section)

- **connect and group dates together** – this is particularly helpful for people who have completed a range of short term roles over several years when travelling or meeting family commitments – it also eliminates date gaps which can make decision makers nervous because they can incorrectly imagine that you may have been lazy, sick, on drugs, in court, in jail etc – and you may have just been on parental leave!)

- **cover all dates in your experience section but provide useful descriptions for specific time gaps** – you may have actually chosen to take a break and you can use a variety of words to cover this time frame – sabbatical, research, writing, studying, travelling etc. You may not have had a specific role or employer, but you can provide information about what you were doing during this time

- **provide full disclosure but be tactful** – as I mentioned in Section 3.1, I had a client who had spent some time in jail for white collar crime and he now provides corporate consulting services. He could not, in good faith, leave these details off of his LinkedIn Profile because his clients can easily find this information via a Google search. He regularly tells people that spending time in jail was helpful to his professional career and he also learnt to cook and completed other studies. This information makes his LinkedIn Profile interesting and informative. If he had been in jail for a different crime, he could list the name of the Holding Company of the prison as the 'Company Name' and his 'Title' could have been Kitchen Hand, Administration etc. It is not a lie, but it does help showcase the positive rather than the negative

- **add professional development to the Education section** – if you have not had very much formal education, or it was a long time ago, you could include comprehensive details of workshops, professional development or courses in the Education section (even day sessions) to ensure your LinkedIn Profile is more up to date

- **ensure that all of your social media profiles are consistent** – if you have any other social media profiles, you should make sure that they have a consistent look and feel, with the same message, primary and secondary keywords and signals if they are part of your overall digital footprint trying to achieve your purpose. If you try and represent yourself in one way on LinkedIn and you appear as something entirely different on Facebook, you are confusing the 'message' you are sending to the marketplace

If you are helping someone else to overcome their past challenges, please do not 'take over' and do everything for them. Make every effort to enable them to take action.

A long time ago, I helped a very close relative get a job and she did not respect the opportunity at all. In fact it was so bad, she actually got sacked! She then asked me to help her get another job and I said, "No, you did not appreciate my help the first time." She grumbled.

She then went on to pursue the career she had always wanted – and has been enjoying her work for the last 25 years!

Just remember, you can 'lead a horse to water, but you cannot make them drink it.' You will help your loved one the most if you help them do what they need to do themselves. If I am approached by a caring person and they ask me to see their loved one (partner, child, friend, colleague etc), I tell them that their loved one has to make the appointment otherwise I will not see them. I know it sounds cruel, but I can tell you, it works!

Action occurs when responsibility is accepted.

Action 55: *Never lie on your LinkedIn Profile, but be tactful how you share some parts of your story*

6.5 Add Some Flair To Your LinkedIn Profile

This book is all about achieving your purpose. There are various ways to personalize your LinkedIn Profile and really give it some zing.

I would like to encourage you to incorporate content that leads the reader to say, in their own mind, 'hell yes' or 'hell no.' If you are really keen to find work, you may not feel confident to do this, but it is essential – so I invite you to be a little courageous!

Why should you do this? Well, it is a great way to eliminate options that won't be suitable for both you and the other person or company. Although you may really want to work, you may not wish to work in certain industries, be managed in a particular way and you might not even fit into a certain enterprise culture.

When you are clear on your purpose, you can provide content that is aligned with your purpose and this content will appeal to people who are on the same wavelength as you or are interested in the value you offer.

By way of example, my LinkedIn Profile was regularly attracting people that I could not assist. They wanted me to provide free advice and assistance to find work and a visa in Australia. Unfortunately, I am not a registered migration agent, so I simply could not help them.

To solve this issue, I have published a huge range of free practical advice online which anyone can easily access by visiting my LinkedIn Profile or my http://sueellson.com website. I have also mentioned my approximate charge out rate in my LinkedIn Summary so now I receive direct contact from people who are ready to book an appointment and they already understand how I will work with them to achieve part of their goals (not do it for them). Everyone wins.

Another LinkedIn Profile I read had me laughing from start to finish. It was written by a person who currently works for the Australian Taxation Office and included a lot of jokes about working for the government. He wasn't looking for a new job and his humorous Summary made that very clear. It was written in the 'first person' as this fitted with his purpose. I found his LinkedIn Profile extremely humorous – and memorable!

You can also add a bit more flair by having a distinctive profile photo and background image (even better if the background image incorporates some of the same color or formatting as your Profile Photo). Carefully select relevant rich media and include interesting details about your past achievements throughout your LinkedIn Profile. A consistent approach to your formatting, especially using short dot points, makes your LinkedIn Profile scan friendly, easy to understand and it helps the reader understand the value you are offering.

You do not have to say what you 'do not' want, you simply need to be clear about what you 'do want.' If someone reads your 'do want' information and what they have to offer is something different, they will not contact you. This saves you both a lot of wasted time and energy.

For example, if you mention some of your Personal Skills in your Summary and they include things like being proactive, people-focused and perceptive, you are probably not suitable for a traditional data entry role. But you could be ideal for a sales, social work or counseling role.

If you are in business, this process eliminates the proverbial tire kickers. These are the people who contact you, ask you lots of questions, waste a lot of your time and never purchase any of your goods or services.

You may also like to think of it this way. There are three types of people. Those people that no matter how good your product or service is, they will not buy it. The second type will buy your product or service in conjunction with you and perhaps take care of some aspect themselves (for example a good relationship with a professional adviser). The third type of person is the one who wants a product or service to do everything for them.

You need to write the content on your LinkedIn Profile for the type of person you want to attract.

Now you could make the false assumption that you never want to reach the first person (who will never buy your product or service). But I am here to tell you that these people can actually be amazing referrers if you treat them well. I personally like working with the second type of person (which is how this book has been written). I will leave someone else to look after the third type of person!

Ironically, if you want a job, the third type of person is often exactly the type of person you want to attract!

Action 56: *Be courageous enough to include some 'hell yes' or 'hell no' content on your LinkedIn Profile to help attract the right opportunity aligned with your purpose and eliminate what you don't want*

6.6 Changing Your Purpose, Job or Enterprise Direction

LinkedIn can also give you an opportunity to change your purpose and change the direction you would like to have in the future.

Some career advisers and resume experts recommend that you only include your last 10 years of experience in your LinkedIn Profile or resume, but I disagree. If someone is going to discriminate against you because of your age and not recognize your value, you don't want to explore that opportunity and waste your time going through the job selection process.

I also believe that my first full time job gave me an enormous range of transferable skills, valuable corporate experience and helped establish excellent behaviors that have served me well throughout my working life.

I have also been able to identify skills (for example, training) that I gained with my first employer that I can still use right now, many years later. By selecting my Primary and Secondary Keywords aligned with my current purpose, I can gain maximum search results value when they are included in a majority of the jobs I have completed throughout the years (but again, I have not lied).

What is even better is that I have been able to re-use some of those skills learned early on in my career, in other roles, so I can re-use those 'on-purpose' keywords throughout my LinkedIn Profile. I can also select secondary keywords that are related to my current purpose and re-align my LinkedIn Profile according to my current purpose if I change my purpose in the future.

I can also de-focus some areas (by reducing the amount of detail in non-related areas) and maximize other areas, without lying. I have also summarized my story in a modern way so that readers can understand what I did in the past and how that relates to my current purpose (if they choose to read it all).

There are also some things that I do not mention. I never say XX years of experience, in any section, under any circumstances. I say this because I remember when I was in my 20's and I distinctly remember not being able to see any of my own future beyond the age of 30. If someone had told me then that they had 20 years of experience in one particular area of expertise, I would have automatically assumed that they were a dinosaur!

On the other hand, if they had simply told me about all of the things that they have done over the last 20 years, I would have seen them as a GURU! You need to think about how you wish to be perceived – as an expert or out of date – and prepare your content accordingly.

You also need to think about how your values may have changed in the recent past. You may have been affected by a traumatic event, a significant life transition or suddenly developed a change in priorities. One of these episodes could have been the catalyst for you buying this book.

You may also want a similar financial reward for your efforts in a completely different field or you may want to work in a different way. If that is the case, re-examine your purpose and be clear about this before making assumptions that only 'other people' have success – you need to adjust your strategies for your purpose.

It may also be unrealistic to expect hero status (or pay) from day one of a new direction that requires a new skill set.

You may also need to go through your transition in stages and ultimately, be realistic about how long it will take to transition to a new area. The good news is that a good strategy will help you get there sooner and if you have an expert on call to help you, it could be even easier than you expect.

Action 57: *If you are changing your purpose, re-focus your LinkedIn content around your future purpose and de-focus some of your past experience, but never lie and be realistic about how long it will take to transition to a new field*

7. Recruitment And Human Resources Practices

I have been fortunate to work within organizations and within recruitment firms and attract, recruit and retain quality staff. From a human resources (HR) perspective, I have been able to identify the needs of the enterprise and match them with suitable hiring practices. I have also managed staff and supported the HR industry through my involvement with the Australian Human Resources Institute http://ahri.com.au. I have also worked with many individuals who are part of outplacement and expatriate transition programs.

Over the years, I have noticed a gradual increase in organizational compliance as enterprises have had to implement policies and procedures around affirmative action, diversity, access and equity, gender equality, health and safety, bullying, parental leave, social media protocols etc.

Not surprisingly, I believe that the LinkedIn Platform has made a difference to the recruitment and human resources aspects of enterprises today.

This section is mainly written for people in recruitment and human resources, but if you are a potential employee, understanding these topics can help you select the best strategies for your purpose.

Action 58: *Understand how recruitment and human resources practices can affect the strategies you select to achieve your purpose*

7.1 Perceived LinkedIn Risks To Enterprises

Recruiters and HR Professionals are often asked questions by enterprises about how LinkedIn affects their organization. Here I will list some of the most common perceived risks.

Poaching

One of the most common concerns I hear from business is, 'Won't everyone else try and poach my staff if I encourage my staff to have a LinkedIn Profile?'

The world of work is constantly changing – and people have been 'poached' from organizations long before LinkedIn was created in 2003. Yes, it makes people easier to find, but it also encourages enterprises to improve their offerings to keep good quality talent. One of the simplest things a manager can do is regularly and authentically, say thank you and acknowledge the employee's contribution (or the client's business).

Fake Profiles

Most con artists have worked out multiple ways to source money from unsuspecting victims. Just because the content is on LinkedIn does not mean that it is necessarily verified and 100% correct – so please, remember to stick to standard business security and due diligence procedures.

LinkedIn also has a range of security procedures designed to detect and report spammers – but this does not stop people lying on their LinkedIn Profile.

Connections

I encourage individuals who work in sales or who have a very high profile in the community or their organization (celebrity, politician, business leader) to change one of their LinkedIn Settings http://linkedin.com/settings/summary – 'Select who can see your connections' and change this to 'Only You.' This provides a small safety net for poaching clients or making assumptions about a person's influence or networks. As always, align this setting with your purpose or the purpose of the enterprise you represent.

If you are from the 'old school' you may decide that you don't want anyone else to see who you are connected to (for various business and personal reasons). If you are in the 'new school' you may realize that there is abundance in the world and enough for everyone so sharing that information could actually be helpful to you.

There is no right or wrong answer, but making this choice in a conscious way based on your purpose is important.

Databases

Every enterprise should have a social media policy about how Connections sourced via LinkedIn through a current job are added to the enterprise's records.

Each enterprise should have 'one source of truth' and if there is an in-house Customer Relationship Management (CRM) system, then new Connections sourced via LinkedIn should not only be made with currently employed individuals, they should be added to the in-house database. This way, when the employee leaves the enterprise, the Connections are not lost.

Time Wasting

Every individual, manager and enterprise owner knows that time can easily be wasted (via LinkedIn or any other distraction). That is why there is such a strong emphasis in this book on achieving your purpose. Your purpose needs to be clearly understood before spending any time on LinkedIn because if it is not clear at the beginning, minutes can quickly become hours and not deliver the results you need.

By focusing on your intention, you will get results. If any procedure takes longer than 10 minutes and you become 'stuck,' it is time to stop and get some help! Time wasting can be reduced with a defined purpose, a good quality Style Guide and appropriate management and maintenance.

Branding

When an employee lists their current job on their LinkedIn Profile, it is helpful if the employer provides a suggested format to describe that role. I like to suggest that for every role you have had, you include a description of the organization, a list of the tasks and achievements in that role and the website address of the organization (and perhaps your contact details).

If you are part of an enterprise and would like some consistency in how your enterprise is represented online, it would be a good idea to provide the enterprise description and format you recommend for your employee's LinkedIn Profile and provide this information during the Induction or Onboarding Process.

Former Employees

One particular organization in regional Victoria has a range of employees who no longer work for the enterprise but they still list the enterprise as their current employer. This essentially makes it easier for the person to find another job (it is easier to go from employment to employment rather than unemployment to employment), but it is incorrect.

Enterprises need to have a process that ensures former employees update their online LinkedIn Profile within a reasonable time of their departure (I would suggest a maximum of six weeks).

Recommendations

Again, enterprises need to make a decision on whether or not colleagues and supervisors can provide Recommendations on LinkedIn whilst they work for the enterprise. Ideally, this needs to be discussed and confirmed in writing at the start of employment. If Recommendations are allowed but certain comments cannot be made for legal reasons, this information needs to be provided in writing and confirmed as received.

Digital Disruption

In many ways, LinkedIn has been a game-changer for recruitment and human resources. It has helped decision makers find people, complete due diligence research, verify knowledge, skills and networks, review recommendations, collect social proof and gather intelligence 24 hours a day, seven days a week, internationally via a computer or mobile device.

It has significantly reduced the number of recruitment consultants who have previously written advertisements, processed applications and short listed candidates.

It has enabled enterprises to reach out directly to future hires and attract quality candidates if they have excellent talent attraction and management techniques (good career branding material, timely recruitment processes, excellent induction processes).

Like all areas of modern life, it is constantly evolving. Consider this, Digital Disruption has already happened because the:

- world's largest taxi company doesn't own taxis (Uber)

- world's largest accommodation provider doesn't own real estate (AirBNB)

- world's largest hotel booking websites are not run by travel agents (Booking, Trivago, Expedia)

- world's largest phone companies don't own telecommunications infrastructure (Skype, WeChat)

- world's most valuable retailer doesn't have inventory (Alibaba)

- world's most popular media owner doesn't create content (Facebook)

- world's fastest growing banks don't have actual money (SocietyOne)

- world's largest movie house doesn't own any cinemas (Netflix)

- world's largest software vendors don't write the apps (Apple and Google)

I am not alarmed – in my view, we just need to re-think how we operate. In the 'good old days,' these go-betweens did exist, just in a different format.

For example, wholesalers would distribute products from suppliers and deliver to retailers. Salespeople would sell retail products but never make them. Media outlets would produce content – but they were paid by classified advertisements.

Essentially, many of the same processes are still occurring, just in a slightly different format – and there is still opportunity available as you can be sure that even the models we have now will change again in the future.

See if you can relate to the old ways and the new ways like this:

Concept	Old Way	New Way
Strategy	Efficiency	Innovation
Culture	Hierarchy	Collaboration
Talent	Low Cost	High Skill
Technology Adoption	Default to No	Default to Yes
Technology Usage	Legacy, Location Based	Cloud, Mobile, Apps
User Experience	We Know What's Best	Users Know What's Best
Project Management	Sequential	Adaptive
Business Model	Service and Support	Relationship and Partner

* `Original source Michael Krigsman and slightly modified*

In my view, many of these changes are for the better!

Action 59: *Identify any risks associated with your enterprise or job search process and adjust your strategy to achieve your purpose*

7.2 How To Interpret LinkedIn Profiles

I once read a very funny Post on Pulse by a Sydney writer who made the claim that the only people who have a good quality LinkedIn Profile are the people who work in sales! He claimed that the successful people were actually out there in the real world doing the work!

To be fair, I am quite sure that there are many extremely successful people living their lives without a LinkedIn Profile. But I have also helped many other people secure amazing opportunities with a LinkedIn Profile that was tailored for their purpose.

If you are the only person in your niche in your location with an optimized LinkedIn Profile, you are in a very good position! Alternatively, if there is a lot of competition in your niche in your location, you need to make sure that your LinkedIn Profile stands out to the exact people within your target audience (and have faith – you are unique and most people still have personal preferences!).

As I have reviewed thousands of resumes and LinkedIn Profiles over the years, there are some general items I review and assess when reading the content for the first time.

- **Photo** – it is obvious, but it should be of good quality and aligned with the person's purpose, ultimately, it showcases a certain level of self-respect

- **Headline** – I prefer it to include keywords, but if it is just their current position, if they are a technical expert, I excuse this faux pas. If it is too 'salesy', I stop immediately

- **Connections** – I look for a minimum of 60 connections – I find that people with less than this number are usually spammers. I review shared connections (which will always be visible) and sometimes other connections to make a further assessment about their integrity

- **Summary** – I like to see some useful information in this section – and more than one sentence (which can make them appear lazy). If it is clear and concise and could be used as a professional biography for an introduction as a speaker, this is very helpful

- **Completeness** – I like to see a reasonable level of detail in a LinkedIn Profile. I do understand that many people are uncomfortable sharing their story publicly, but they do need to at least fill in the absolute basics in a consistent manner, without spelling mistakes and preferably, using capitals and lower case in the most professional way (but never all capital letters as this is classified as 'shouting' in the online world)

- **Languages** – although I only speak English and a tiny bit of French, I do believe that people who have learnt more than one language do have something 'extra' to offer (even if they only have an Elementary level of proficiency)

- **Advice for Contacting** – Even if the person is extremely well known, if they can provide a link to an online 'form' so that I can still reach them, I find this impressive. For everyone else, I believe it is a good idea to have a clear message here and as a minimum, include a personal email address (but put some spaces around the @ symbol so that your email address is not picked up by spam robots). If you are in job search mode, include your mobile phone number in the international dialing format (+61 402 222 333) so that people can reach you immediately (and press the number if they are viewing the profile from a mobile device)

- **Endorsements** – I only give these a cursory overview – but I do like to check if the skills endorsed match the rest of their LinkedIn Profile story

- **Recommendations** – I like to see six or more, and not all in the last month, from a variety of past roles – both colleagues and supervisors (not fellow students!)

- **Bling** – as mentioned before, I do encourage everyone to add some rich media (images, videos, animated gifs, presentations etc.) to their LinkedIn Profile – but not too much as that can make the person look like they are trying too hard and can be off-putting – be selective

- **Length of Employment** – if the person is constantly job hopping across multiple industries or locations, I get very nervous that they will do the same in the next job. However, I always put this in context depending on the nature of their work or the reason for their constant changes (for example, they could be an expatriate trailing spouse or an IT contractor and these jobs are usually short term)

- **Types of Organisations** – if the person has recently worked in one organisation for more than 10 years and describes their role in a language only understood by that industry and cannot reveal transferable skills or knowledge, I would be reluctant to consider them for a change of direction. They are typecasting themselves if they do not explain their story in a language their target audience understands

- **Reading between the lines** – this is a skill that I have personally developed over the years and it is a combination of many factors. I look for date gaps, language style, formatting, titles, companies, connections etc. as a collective concept and look for congruence or conflict. I can infer a lot about someone's personality and style and make a reasonably quick assessment and if they are a 'borderline' choice, I would always investigate further

- **Other LinkedIn Profiles are quickly classified as '40 footers'** – I wouldn't touch them with a 40 foot barge pole! These are the ones I usually decline when I receive an invitation to connect, especially if they haven't even looked at my LinkedIn Profile and they are in some far off country in an obscure role and have less than 20 connections etc.

Naturally every decision maker has a different way to assess the content of a LinkedIn Profile. Your goal is to make sure that the LinkedIn Profiles you assess ultimately lead to you achieving your purpose as a decision maker. If you are trying to convince a decision maker, you need to make sure that it 'speaks' to them.

Action 60: *Understand what you need to look for when assessing your own or others LinkedIn Profiles*

7.3 How To Find Quality Candidates Via Advanced Search

Whether you are looking for candidates through your own LinkedIn network or through a tool like LinkedIn Recruiter, you need to be savvy in your approach.

A database is only as good as the content that is in it. LinkedIn is a very large international database, so there is a very good chance that you will find some good candidates, particularly if you are looking for professionals currently earning over $100,000 per year. You may also find that it is necessary to use LinkedIn and some other sources to find the right candidates for your needs.

My next door neighbor has been in recruitment for many years and he recently told me a very interesting story. He had been given a recruitment assignment to find someone with a very specific skill set. He ultimately found this person and they were on LinkedIn, but he did not find them via LinkedIn – because this person had not completed their LinkedIn Profile in full and his keywords were not included.

It actually took my neighbor six weeks to find the successful candidate. It took several phone calls, meetings, a lot of research and investigation.

A typical decision maker in an enterprise does not necessarily have these recruitment skills, so yes, it is still sometimes necessary to hire a recruitment consultant to help you find quality candidates.

If the recruitment consultant only finds one person worthy of an in-house interview, trust their skills and please don't insist that you waste two other people's time by interviewing them if they have already been reviewed by the recruiter and classified as unsuitable.

You outsourced the recruitment role to them, so why repeat the work you have already delegated?

LinkedIn is an amazing research tool. As I have mentioned earlier, one of the best ways to find work or business is by referral – so by starting with people in your network who are related in some way to the person or skills you are seeking, you may be able to be referred to the right candidate.

If you are the candidate who wants to be found, remember to fill in your LinkedIn Profile!!! Some of the best talent in the world has some of the worst details on LinkedIn!

If you start to do some Advanced LinkedIn searches and find that there are actually a number of people who come up in search results, you may wish to refine your searches to find someone more closely aligned to your requirements.

For this reason, I often like to include technical competency keywords as well as job descriptions in my keyword searches – for example Senior Project Manager + Agile + PRINCE2 and also choose a location and a specific radius. I usually only use the keywords box and specify the location as these seem to bring up the best LinkedIn Search Results.

If I happen to find someone I already know in my search results, I will often revisit their LinkedIn Profile. When I do, it may also show me the 'People Also Viewed' box and this can often lead to interesting possibilities and worthwhile discussions.

Some of the LinkedIn Premium Products http://linkedin.com/premium/products also enable you to send Sponsored Messages to people with certain LinkedIn Profiles. I have received some interesting direct invitations from all over the world in this manner, but as a potential candidate, I have to say that I prefer a direct approach rather than a bulk approach, particularly when I have already included my contact details on my LinkedIn Profile.

Action 61: *Select comprehensive keyword search strings for Advanced Searches on LinkedIn to find quality candidates and approach people directly for the best results*

7.4 Posting Job Ads On LinkedIn

As a decision maker, you can post a job ad on LinkedIn. You can do it individually with a Job Post http://linkedin.com/job/consumer/common

Post/displayNewJob via your own LinkedIn Profile or you can sign up for the more comprehensive Job Slots http://business.linkedin.com/talent-solutions/post-jobs

There are also other Talent finding services including LinkedIn Recruiter http://business.linkedin.com/talent-solutions/recruiter if you are doing a lot of recruitment. Your enterprise may also like to consider a Company Career Page http://business.linkedin.com/talent-solutions/company-career-pages or Work With Us Ads http://business.linkedin.com/talent-solutions/job-ads

These packages offer various levels of promotion – as an advertisement, directly targeted to candidates, through the LinkedIn Job Search App http://linkedin.com/mobile etc.

If you want your job advertisements to attract good quality candidates, you need to produce good quality advertisements. To ensure that your job ad will be searchable, you will need to make a choice for all of the selections where there is a drop down box and I encourage you to provide detailed information in the 'Job Description' section.

If you believe you are likely to attract a lot of candidates, it is a good idea to include a specific task in the job advertisement – for example, you could ask candidates to include certain specific information in their application – this will also help differentiate between the 'genuinely interested candidates' and the 'prospecting for any job 'candidates.

LinkedIn enables you to either receive applications through LinkedIn or redirect candidates to your website. If you choose your own website, it is a good idea to ask candidates when they apply how they found out about the role so that you can determine how many have come through via LinkedIn.

If you are interested in receiving applications from people currently living in other locations, encourage them to explain why they are interested in the role and how they will secure the relevant work rights or visa.

An essential component of effective recruitment in today's marketplace is responding in a very timely manner to applicants. If you can contact your applicants within 24 hours and make a hiring decision within seven days, you will impress them with your efficiency and create an excellent first impression which is likely to lead to a good quality working relationship. If they are not successful but still have a good experience through the recruitment process, this is an excellent branding exercise for your enterprise.

Additional assistance and advice is available from LinkedIn sales staff and you can also book demonstrations of the various LinkedIn Talent Solutions online via http://business.linkedin.com/talent-solutions.

Personally, I always recommend a recruitment strategy that aligns with your target audience and your purpose. So ultimately, this may or may not include advertising through LinkedIn (but I would always recommend that you conduct some Advanced Searches via LinkedIn).

If you are a decision maker or HR manager and you choose to work in conjunction with a Recruitment Consultant, I encourage you to choose a Recruitment Consultant who has been in the industry for more than three years.

Recruitment Consultants are often paid on a commission basis after a candidate has been in the designated role for more than three months. Consultants who are still in the industry after three years are more likely to have gained the essential wisdom they need to source and secure quality candidates on a regular basis.

If you are a Recruitment Consultant, I encourage you to secure a recruitment certification through a professional association and also make sure that your LinkedIn Profile is befitting a recruitment expert. If you are an in-house enterprise recruiter, keep up your professional development education and also consider securing a recruitment or human resources certification.

Action 62: *Whilst there are various ways to advertise jobs on LinkedIn, to attract the best candidates, prepare quality advertisements and if you are working with a trusted Recruitment Consultant, listen to their advice*

7.5 Preparing For Job Interviews

A job candidate should always research an organization before applying for a job and attending a job interview. Likewise, an interviewer should do some research on a job applicant before their job interview.

Good quality interviewers will ensure that they ask every short listed candidate the same questions and perhaps a few extras related to that particular candidate. Behavioral interview questions are very common nowadays – questions that include 'tell me about a time when'….as they provide information about past behavior which is a general indicator of future behavior.

95% of decision makers will now do a 'Google Search' before offering a job to a candidate. Around 85% of employers say a positive online reputation influences their hiring decision.

This is part of the due diligence process and they will be assessing the person's digital footprint. They may also visit Facebook and other social media platforms. I would like to suggest that rather than complete a 'cursory glance' after a job interview, it is a good idea to view this information before the job interview and ask the candidate questions based on the content you find.

For example, a good quality LinkedIn Profile will be fully completed and hopefully, include the details of at least one project. If you ask a question related to this project in a job interview, you can request more detail but also assess whether the story matches what they have on their LinkedIn Profile. It also shows that you are genuinely interested in the candidate.

If you have received a resume, you should also check that the dates on both the LinkedIn Profile and the Resume match. If the person has some Recommendations on their LinkedIn Profile, read these in detail and also visit the LinkedIn Profile of the person providing the Recommendation.

If a formal Certification or Accreditation is required for the job, you may also like to check with the Governing Body that the person has the Certification or Accreditation that they have listed on their LinkedIn Profile (unfortunately some people do lie on their LinkedIn Profile).

If you share some Connections with the candidate and you have a good relationship with that shared Connection, you may even want to discuss this in the job interview and ask the candidate if you can call the shared Connection before making your final recruitment decision (along with any supplied Referees).

When you visit the candidate's LinkedIn Profile, they may also have some website links in the 'Contact Info' section – these may link to a personal blog or website which may also be worth reviewing. I did this for a potential Award Recipient and his blog completely contravened his Award Application and was actually a potential threat to the integrity of the Awards process.

You may also like to save the person's LinkedIn Profile photograph to your computer, go to Google, choose Images and then click on the picture of a camera, upload the image and do a reverse image search to see where else the photograph appears online. This process can be very revealing!

If you type the person's name into Google and then a space, you can see if their name is associated with any other Google search query. For instance, if you start typing "Sue Ellson" you will see that people often type my name and then the words 'linkedin,' 'newcomers network' or 'open forum.'

Essentially, LinkedIn can be a great way to provide access to other digital content for your potential candidate, so it is well worthwhile reviewing the LinkedIn Profile in a bit more detail before a job interview.

Action 63: *Utilize LinkedIn as a tool to explore a candidate's digital footprint either before or after a job interview*

7.6 Inducting New Employees

After the initial excitement of receiving a job offer, the Induction or Onboarding process during the first few days and weeks of a new employment relationship is very important – and once again, LinkedIn needs to be discussed.

Most enterprises now have a Social Media Policy and this needs to be provided in writing and the new hire should ask questions if they need any clarification and then sign and date their acceptance of these terms and conditions.

This is an ideal opportunity to explain the enterprise's branding and communications strategy and invite the new hire to update their LinkedIn Profile accordingly. The policy may provide a description of the enterprise that should be used in the Experience Section, an official Job Title and a Position Description that can be used in any online content published by the new employee and so on.

There may be a protocol around selecting who can see your Connections (particularly if the new employee is in business development, sales or an executive position). There may be a recommended background photo option and a request to follow the Company Page and join a relevant LinkedIn Group for any parent or sister enterprises.

During employment, there may also be requirements to share details of new Connections on LinkedIn with the in-house database, particularly if those new Connections have been established via their employment activities. Details of achievements or projects with commercially sensitive information should not be published online (perhaps percentages could be used rather than dollar amounts).

There may also be a component related to Performance Appraisal, Rewards or Recognition.

If your employee receives an Honor or Award during their employment, this is worth recording on their LinkedIn Profile.

It is also necessary to decide on a policy in relation to Syncing email addresses with LinkedIn. If a work email address is synced with

LinkedIn, copies of email correspondence will end up with LinkedIn. Individuals can decide if they would like to do this with their personal email address but it is probably not appropriate to do this with a work email address.

The Social Media Policy should also include details of what needs to be done when the employment relationship ends and this needs to be discussed at the start of the employment relationship. How soon after departure must the LinkedIn Profile be updated (recording that the job has ended)? Does any correspondence sent through LinkedIn need to be forwarded to the enterprise? What other records, job ads, posts etc., need to be transferred?

Whilst it would be nice to let 'common sense prevail,' if these topics are not discussed at the beginning of an employment relationship, it can be difficult to obtain agreement later on in an employment relationship. If you are currently working in an enterprise and would like to implement some of these suggestions, I would recommend that you do so with an appropriate and well managed change management initiative.

Action 64: *LinkedIn needs to be included in an enterprise's Social Media Policy with specific instructions for LinkedIn Profile content, activity and processes confirmed at the start of the employment relationship*

7.7 LinkedIn For Leaders, Managers And Employees

The old rules of business had proverbial 'players' keeping their cards 'close to their chest.' Business was largely a secretive affair completed behind closed doors and success usually involved keeping information in an exclusive format, well away from employees and reserved exclusively for managers and executives.

Our society has been transformed with technology and education. Now more than ever, you can access a huge amount of information, simply by typing a few words in to Google. Some years ago, someone told me that there is 'no such thing as a new idea.' I was devastated! I genuinely believed that I had come up with a few good ideas that were brand new – but if I think about it a little more carefully, they are essentially ideas based on other ideas – so most people are simply building on existing concepts. Now I can truly admire those original inventors!

The other way that life has transformed is that the power of selected individuals has shifted and society has become much more democratic. In the past, content published in the print media was largely controlled by editors and sub-editors.

Now, almost anyone can publish content on social media, forums and websites. Even printing a paper flyer or poster is relatively cheap (although the readership cannot be guaranteed). Digital content can quickly become viral and can have serious consequences.

So now there are experts in 'crisis management.' The good news is, that most of these crises last about 18 hours…so if you can respond appropriately within this time frame, you will be able to learn the lesson and move on.

The other side of this argument is the benefit that can be derived from social media. A well designed branding and communications strategy can see all of your employees as brand advocates and ambassadors for your enterprise. Messages they post can be spread through their networks and provide referrals and brand recognition. They can also utilize their networks for information and intelligence gathering.

One major bank in Australia originally banned access to social media on the work computers, but they changed their mind when they realized that the productivity and the performance of the organization increased when employees had access to social media!

I am not suggesting a free-for-all without guidelines. Just as each person needs to think about their own purpose, each enterprise needs to think about their purpose and how this can be achieved through all of their resources, in an ethical and effective manner.

For some enterprises, this is a new way of working. Some senior managers and executives have a great deal of business acumen, but poor skills in the area of social media. If the enterprise has decided to utilize LinkedIn as part of their business strategy, it is ESSENTIAL that this direction be adopted by management.

It could be necessary to organize additional training and personalized coaching for managers and leaders (and I have conducted these sessions across Australia). They will need to lead by example –

and as an absolute minimum, they must have a good quality personal LinkedIn Profile. Once the leaders have updated their 'real estate' online, then the strategy can be implemented across the enterprise – starting with the LinkedIn Company Page.

Leading from the bottom up of the enterprise with social media is usually less effective at generating results because it may not be aligned with the overall enterprise strategy or incorporate the business acumen and professional wisdom of the leaders.

Eric Hoffer put it quite wisely when he said, "Every new adjustment is a crisis in self-esteem."

Action 65: *Leaders and Managers need to be the first employees to update their LinkedIn Profile and supervise the content on the Company Page to ensure that the enterprise's online content and communications are aligned with the enterprise's strategy*

7.8 LinkedIn For Leaving Employees

As mentioned in Section 7.5, when a new employee is hired, the details of the Social Media Policy need to be shared, signed and dated at the start of their employment relationship. When they leave the enterprise, the correct processes need to be carried out at the end of the employment relationship.

Exit interviews, dismissals, terminations and farewells can all be stressful. So as you can imagine, if the employee knows what to expect at the end of the employment relationship from the beginning of the employment relationship, it is much easier to implement the necessary processes at the end of the employment relationship.

Although the written Social Media Policy may have been provided previously, it may be necessary to remind the departing employee of the specific requirements with LinkedIn. These can include:

- adding the final date of employment to their Experience section

- joining the alumni group if you have one (popular in consulting firms)

- sharing the details of the Connections sourced throughout their employment with the in-house database

- withdrawing from any Closed Employee Only LinkedIn Group

- reminding them about the enterprise policy in relation to Recommendations and provide one or more Recommendations from selected employees, managers or leaders if this is part of the enterprise Social Media Policy

- updating their LinkedIn Profile with what they have achieved in their role (without revealing commercially sensitive information)

- adding in details of any Courses completed throughout their employment

- removing their work email address from their LinkedIn Profile (very few organisations monitor this)

- sending through a copy of any correspondence sent via LinkedIn that needs to be forwarded to the enterprise as a backup copy

- transferring any other records, job ads etc.

- updating any Posts they may have been published on LinkedIn in their previous role/s with your enterprise

- confirming a date for the completion of these tasks (usually within six weeks but preferably before departure so that it can be verified immediately)

- asking them if there is any way they would like to continue to support the enterprise online in the future

- explaining the consequences of any non-compliance (initially, try and manage this process politely and with direct personal contact phone calls rather than formal written demands)

The goal of this process is to end the employment relationship on good terms and also protect the interests of the enterprise. If this is done well, the former employee can continue to be an enterprise referrer, advocate and ambassador and be able to be on call in the future as part of the enterprise's extended family.

They will forever remain listed as an 'employee' on LinkedIn if the enterprise has a Company Page.

Action 66: *Design effective LinkedIn processes for departing employees to ensure that they remain enterprise referrers, advocates and ambassadors in the future*

7.9 LinkedIn For Former Employees

Your former employees can be a great source of referrals, information, intelligence and general branding as referrers, advocates and ambassadors.

Some of the best recruits to an organization come via a referral from an existing or former employee. Some employees leave for family or personal development reasons (perhaps even some international experience or further study) and welcome an opportunity to return to the enterprise at a later date.

Every effort should be made to maintain quality relationships with former employees. To value them for their contribution and wish them well in their future endeavors.

If they have left and are now a 'competitor,' this should inspire your enterprise to constantly evolve and adapt, not participate in retaliatory behavior. Remember that business is always changing and customers and clients have always had the option to go elsewhere.

Alumni programs have traditionally been associated with educational facilities, but many leading enterprises understand the latent value and opportunity that former employees offer to the existing enterprise. If your enterprise has a LinkedIn University Profile (because you are a training provider, school, college or university), then you really must make every effort to engage effectively with your Alumni as you have additional tools available through LinkedIn.

If you have a large enough number of former employees to create an enterprise alumni LinkedIn Closed Group, this can be a great way to make these former employees feel valued and keep them informed about what is happening now in the enterprise. I would recommend that your enterprise share an update in the Group at least once a month. Also, you can still encourage them to keep following your Company Profile even if you do not have an Alumni Group.

Selected VIP former employees may also be put on a 'reminder' schedule and contacted personally up to three times a year to maintain the 'connection' with your enterprise. This role could be delegated to the Marketing or Executive Suite of the enterprise.

Action 67: *Consider creating a LinkedIn alumni strategy for former employees to continue your relationship and source quality referrals, information and intelligence in the future*

8. Business and Social Enterprise

I have been involved in a plethora of large and small, for profit and not for profit enterprises over many years. The most successful enterprises are the ones that are clear on their purpose, they meet the needs of their target audience, they operate in the most effective and efficient way possible and they are always keeping themselves up to date and adjusting to the changing needs of their target market.

The least successful enterprises are the ones that adopt an ad hoc approach and are not focused on achieving results and believe that every person wants what they offer. It is very easy to be busy. It is much harder to be productive. Most busy people are not operating according to their purpose.

I have often wished that some not for profit enterprises could be more business-like and that some businesses could have more of a social conscience! Let's hope that both types of enterprises can learn from each other in the future.

A quick question for you. What is the difference between being self-employed and in business? Scale and Leverage. In a business, you have the ability to continually increase your capacity. That said, some people choose self-employment for lifestyle reasons – but they adopt a business approach and thanks to technology can still up-scale and leverage many aspects of their offerings – which is perfectly valid in our internationally connected world (and for the record, that is what I have chosen!).

Either way, whether you are part of a small or large collective of people working for profit or not for profit, there are a range of LinkedIn strategies that can help an enterprise achieve results.

Action 68: *To maintain enterprise success, you need to be clear on your purpose, meet the needs of your target audience, operate effectively and adjust over time*

8.1 Establishing Quality Enterprise Real Estate On LinkedIn

Most enterprises have more than one digital profile online. For a start, most enterprises now have a website (or a listing on Google or a directory website). I recommend a LinkedIn Profile for every individual and every enterprise. I do not necessarily recommend an enterprise profile on every other social media platform (although I do always recommend Google+). I recommend LinkedIn because it:

- is likely to come up in search results

- establishes good quality backlinks

- enables individuals to follow the enterprise (via a Newsfeed rather than multiple emails)

- allows you to tell your story in your words

- increases the size of your digital footprint which will lead to developing your digital asset

- is a reputable social media platform

- allows people to do their own due diligence (even though you provide the content)

- provides a broadcast tool (where your content is guaranteed to be published)

- allows like-minded people to find and connect with you

- has an international audience that is constantly expanding

- keeps reinventing itself (so it is likely to be around for a long time)

- has new features that are constantly being added (Pulse, SlideShare, Lynda, Connectifier)

- can publish search engine optimized content

Unfortunately, I have seen a lot of poor quality enterprise Company Pages.

There are some essential strategies that I recommend for enterprise Company Pages (online real estate):

- add good quality logos in the dimensions requested (which are also consistent with the logos that appear on your business website and other social media)

Sue Ellson

- provide a good quality description with your primary and secondary keywords designed for your target audience that showcases your value and includes your key message, a call to action (and special offer?) and contact details (up to 2,000 characters)

- include the various specialties you have

- fill in all of the other requested information (Founded, Operating Status, Industry etc)

- delete any duplicate LinkedIn Company Pages set up by former employees

- ensure that you have one administrator who knows what they are doing and more than one manager to help manage the Company Page

- share an informative update (not just a sales message) at least once a month

- keep a record of your statistics (for example, your number of Followers) to measure your return on investment (also see Section 8.7)

- invite all of your employees to Follow the Company Page (a study by BrightEdge http://brightedge.com found that 9 out of the top 10 brands with the most Followers on LinkedIn have at least 60% of their employees on LinkedIn. This is an enormously untapped option for showcasing your company profile via other people's LinkedIn Profiles)

- invite all of your employees to like, comment or share Updates from the Company Page

- ensure that all of your existing and former employees have 'chosen' your Company Page from the drop down list as their Employer in the Experience section of their LinkedIn Profile

- invite employees to link to your enterprise website in the list of websites in the 'Contact Info' section of their individual LinkedIn Profiles

- ensure that all of your existing and former employees describe their role with your Company in a consistent manner – with a description of the enterprise, tasks, achievements and your website address (another backlink!)

- if you feature employees on your enterprise website, consider linking to their Customized LinkedIn Profile URL for further information

- prepare a Style Guide for all LinkedIn content produced by the enterprise

Remember that complete Company Profiles have a much better chance of appearing in LinkedIn and Google Search Results. If your description can explain the challenges your products or services solve, include ways to overcome the three most frequent objections and explain how you are unique, you will be well on your way.

You could also consider creating up to ten Showcase Pages. Once you are on your LinkedIn Company Page, there is a blue box on the top right hand side of your screen that has a drop down menu and it allows you to create a Showcase Page. This will create a live page on LinkedIn that is highly optimized – whatever you name the page, it becomes your URL e.g. http://linkedin.com/company/description-appears-here – so if you are trying to optimize individual products or services online, this feature could be useful to you and send out the right signal to either LinkedIn or Google.

That said, it does mean that you then have to go through the process of sharing Updates here and maintaining this profile as well, so it is not always my first recommendation due to the extra time required.

If you are self-employed, you can still create a Company Page provided you have an email address in the name of the 'Company.' For example, I have the email address sueellson@sueellson.com and I have created a Company Page for Sue Ellson at http://linkedin.com/company/2750884 – this allows me to have a 'logo' on my LinkedIn Profile which makes me appear more professional.

Action 69: *Create a quality LinkedIn Company Page for your enterprise and/or select the Company Profile from the drop down list when you enter the organization on your own LinkedIn Profile*

8.2 Building Your Enterprise Digital Asset

Every business needs to have a digital footprint that they eventually build into a digital asset that constantly generates business opportunities. If you have gone through the process of creating a LinkedIn Company Page, make an effort to link to it on your other online content including:

- your business website (either on your About Us or Contact Us page)

- your Google+ Local Business Page (so that you can tell Google where to find your business online)

- your Google+ Personal Profile (so that you can tell Google to present your LinkedIn Company Profile in Google Search Results for your name as content on LinkedIn often performs better than your own website)

- your online trade or membership listings

- your free online directory listings (for example, the former telephone directory type listings)

It is also a good idea to encourage your business clients, suppliers, stakeholders etc to Follow your LinkedIn Company Profile (so that your Company Updates appear in their newsfeed) as well as connect to you personally (particularly if you are the business owner).

If or when you sell or pass on your enterprise, you can include the number of Followers you have on the Company Profile as part of the Asset of your enterprise– and transfer this Following to the new owner (including after your death) – so ultimately, the more Followers your Company Profile has on LinkedIn, the better.

Also remember to record the number of Followers you have on a regular basis (this number is only available as a real time statistic). I do not recommend buying Followers from any source – most social media platforms can detect false Followers.

Action 70: *Add your LinkedIn Company Profile Link to your other online content and aim to increase your Company Followers to build the digital asset of your enterprise*

8.3 Enterprise Updates Via Your LinkedIn Company Profile

LinkedIn generally encourages you to post an Update via your Company Profile every day. I do not recommend this level of frequency, especially in Australia. In my view, it is better to post good quality content less often than poor quality content regularly.

Many enterprise owners are disappointed that their LinkedIn Company Profile doesn't always generate as much interest (via an Update) as their Personal Profile does.

For example, most small business owners have a lot more Connections associated with their Personal Profile and a lot less Followers of their Company Profile so when they send out a personal Update, it goes to a lot more people via a Personal Update than it would if it was sent out as a Company Update.

However, it is extremely important to still post Updates via your Company Profile. Anyone who is conducting thorough due diligence of your business will check you out personally and they will also visit your Company Profile on LinkedIn. If you have three followers but 30 Updates on your LinkedIn Company Profile, it is a lot better than three followers and no Updates.

I would suggest that a minimum schedule for Company Profile Updates would be once a month. What you share will depend upon your purpose and your target audience. The more closely this is aligned, the greater your chance of success.

For example, I provided some consulting advice to a small, but very successful building products company in Melbourne. The CEO had worked in the business for most of his career and had inherited the business from his father and improved and expanded the operation. He hired a university student to create some updates and post them on LinkedIn. They were essentially sales messages, generated zero results and wasted hours of time – all because he thought only young people know how to use social media.

After talking to the CEO for less than 20 minutes, we came up with a range of topics that could have been shared through the LinkedIn Company Page that would have been extremely helpful for his Followers, which included Clients, Suppliers and Architects. He knew the keywords, the content and the useful information that would be of direct benefit to his target audience. All he needed was someone to produce this content, not have someone without any experience in the industry make up something based on some Google research.

It is extremely important to always provide content that is of information or benefit to your target audience – about 70% of the updates should be information based (either new or original content), 20% could be shared from other reputable sources (which will help you appear both knowledgeable and collaborative).

10% can be about any awards, achievements or special offers you have available (sales – if you absolutely must). Depending on your purpose, you could change these ratios, but I would never suggest more than 10% on sales information.

Sharing content on your LinkedIn Company Page will also be helpful if someone visits your Company Page sometime after you have posted the Update – as it provides a brief archive of what has happened in the recent past. Unfortunately there comes a time when your older posts will 'disappear' from LinkedIn.

For this reason, I also encourage you to consider providing an Archive copy of the Updates you have shared via LinkedIn on your Company website as well (perhaps even in your Company Blog). If the updates you share include a link to your website, don't forget that you can also distribute this update through your Google+ profile so that Google can be encouraged to add the details to the Google Search Index.

Action 71: *Choose your enterprise Company Profile Update schedule and make sure that the content you provide is of benefit to your target audience*

8.4 Create A Style Guide For Your Company Updates

It is also a good idea to have a Style Guide for your Company Updates. Think about the following:

- will you use hashtags # to enable your Updates to be found by subject? (hashtags are an indexing tool – they allow viewers to find content that includes the same hashtag and they are very popular on Twitter http://twitter.com and Instagram http://instagram.com)

- will you include a link – to either more details on your website or somewhere else?

- will you make sure that you acknowledge other contributors or enterprises mentioned in the Update (if you type in @ and then their name or Company name, if you are connected to them or following them on LinkedIn, their name will appear on the screen and you can select it and it will 'ping' (notify) them of the item. If they are not on LinkedIn, you could reference their Twitter handle e.g. @sueellson)?

- have you incorporated your primary or secondary keywords?

- will you have a call to action or a special offer?

- will you include a question or ask for comments?

- will you have a rich media component (video, presentation, image etc)?

- will you triple check the wording, spelling and grammar before sharing?

- will you send the Update to all followers or a targeted audience?

- will you vary the style of Updates you share?

- will someone be ready to respond to comments as soon as possible?

- will you review the performance of your updates and modify your behavior?

- will you report on the results to management?

- if the content is particularly successful, will you Sponsor an Update to a wider audience? http://business.linkedin.com/marketing-solutions/products/native-advertising

Action 72: *Create a Style Guide and various processes for your LinkedIn Company Updates*

8.5 Options For Your LinkedIn Social Media Policy

It would be nice to believe that everyone in an enterprise could have basic common sense and ethics in relation to social media. Unfortunately, that is not the case – in fact some people joke that it should be called 'uncommon sense' nowadays because so few people have common sense!

Every enterprise has its own target audience, its own purpose and its own goals. For these reasons, I do not want to be prescriptive about what you should have in your enterprise's social media policy. You will also need to abide by your country's local laws in relation to Employment, Human Resources and Business.

What I will share are some options of what you could include in your Social Media Policy in relation to LinkedIn for employees, managers, directors, advisers and contractors:

- Recruitment Stage

    - view their LinkedIn Profile in Private Mode (via http://linkedin.com/settings/summary – 'Select what others see when you've viewed their profile)

    - check that their resume or CV matches the content on LinkedIn

    - review their Recommendations and cross match with the details they provide for reference checking

    - review their Achievements (if listed) and any Publications (for inappropriate content)

    - review their Endorsements and make sure that the votes are from legitimate experts (not just friends from university)

- view their Recent Activity (blue drop down box on their Profile page) as this will also reveal their number of Followers, and make sure that they have a good track record (particularly if they are in a Communications role)

- review who they are Connected to if their Connections are visible (particularly important for sales roles)

- see if they are part of any enterprise or university Alumni Groups and if they contribute in this area (good for networking)

- make sure they have time to read the LinkedIn Social Media Policy before accepting the role, that they understand what will occur during their relationship with the enterprise and what will happen when they leave and they sign and date it to accept the policy before they start their relationship with you

- Induction or Onboarding Stage

Some of these options could be preferred but optional – but they should at least be discussed during Induction

- ensure that the LinkedIn Social Media Policy has been signed and understood

- ensure that they update their personal LinkedIn Profile in accordance with your requirements and suggested preferences:

- photo format (white or logo background perhaps)

- background format (if you supply an image)

- headline format (if specified by your enterprise)

- experience format (job title, company description, list of tasks, list of achievements, enterprise website address)

- make sure they choose your Company from the drop down box so that the enterprise logo appears on their LinkedIn Profile

- follow your Company on LinkedIn

- encourage them to Connect with selected people in your enterprise (like the CEO or particular Directors etc) and provide them with a list of these people with their LinkedIn URL next to each name

- adding your enterprise website link in their Contact Info section (great backlink strategy)

- join any specified Groups you recommend on LinkedIn

- if they have joined any particular professional association or have a certification that they add this information to their LinkedIn Profile

- that they can add their work email address to their LinkedIn Profile during their relationship but they must remove the email address on the last day of their employment relationship

- that they include any specific keywords in certain locations in their LinkedIn Profile

- that they include a particular call to action and special offer on their LinkedIn Profile

- that they include particular contact information on their LinkedIn Profile (for example, if they are a senior executive, it may be prudent to list the Communications Team email address in the 'Advice for contacting' section)

- explain your enterprise policy in relation to new Connections on LinkedIn whilst they are part of your enterprise (they can Connect but they may also need to add the details to the enterprise CRM)

- explain the Recommendations Policy – whilst they are part of your enterprise, are they allowed to provide Recommendations to other people? Can they only provide personal Recommendations and not discuss the person's performance at your enterprise

- explain the Commercial In Confidence aspects of your enterprise (enterprise information that cannot be shared publicly via LinkedIn – for example, they can discuss achievements in general terms and without figures or details of clients serviced)

- explain how much information they can share with others outside the enterprise (for instance, they may need to keep analytics information private)

- explain that LinkedIn is not a platform for overtly personal content (family photos and jokes) and perhaps encourage stronger privacy settings on other social media platforms (like Facebook)

- explain that they are not allowed to sync their work email address with the LinkedIn Platform (as this will put enterprise information in the LinkedIn Platform)

- let them know who are the Administrators and Managers of the LinkedIn Company Profile and how they can make suggestions to these individuals in the enterprise

- advise them of the internal and external Communications Policy for your enterprise (for example, all enterprise information may need to be distributed via the Communications Team rather than any particular individual in the enterprise)

- explain your policy in relation to any form of bullying, defamation, uncomfortable inference, maliciously false, abusive, threatening, derogatory or defamatory comments about the enterprise, clients or staff etc and your zero tolerance of this behavior

- explain your policy in relation to irate or disgruntled enterprise customers and requests from the media and how this should be dealt with

- explain what statistics they need to provide to the enterprise (for example, you may record how many Connections they have when they start with the enterprise and how many they have when they leave the enterprise – but I would add, that I do not believe it is ethical for you to ask them to delete any of these Connections at the end of your relationship but it is appropriate for them to add the details of certain Connections to the enterprise CRM system)

- discuss how they can support the enterprise on LinkedIn (liking, commenting, sharing Updates, providing referrals to Human Resources, identifying good quality content for the Communications Team etc

- provide details of the enterprise Brand or Style Guidelines for Updates, Posts, Discussions, Connection requests etc

- Relationship Stage

Now that they are a part of your enterprise, you will need to:

- ensure they have procedures for monitoring their activity (most important if they are an Administrator or Manager for the enterprise Company Profile) – perhaps there is a policy that all Updates or Posts need to be checked by a second person before publication

- continuously collect certain statistics (like number of Company Followers, Group Members etc) – it is important that your hires understand that this data is being collected so that they can contribute to the success of the enterprise

- have a system for recognizing and rewarding favorable behavior on LinkedIn (personal acknowledgments for enterprise supporting content publication or sharing or good quality referrals)

- keep everyone informed about the overall enterprise LinkedIn strategy and performance so that they can continue to support it personally

- keep the lines of communication open so that if some content is published or some challenging behavior occurs and this could affect the enterprise in a negative manner, the hired person feels comfortable contacting the necessary person within the enterprise so that the issue can be dealt with as soon as possible in a professional manner (particularly important when a crisis occurs and the media starts contacting individuals)

- ensure that there is a process for dealing with contraventions of the LinkedIn Social Media Policy that is fair and solution based

- encourage hires to publish certain agreed content via LinkedIn (for example, details of Publications or Projects that are suitable for public consumption)

- if sharing views of a personal opinion, make this very clear and make sure that all details supplied are factually correct

- always aim to add value and if it is necessary, be ready to apologize in accordance with enterprise protocols

- don't spam or act outside of the LinkedIn User Agreement, especially if the person is an enterprise Administrator or Manager for the Company Profile

• Ending Relationship Stage

Regardless of how the relationship with a person or enterprise is ending (termination, dismissal, retrenchment, resignation, end of contract, end of project etc), there are some actions that can be included in an enterprise LinkedIn Social Media Policy:

- update the Experience section stating the final month (to be done either immediately or within three months of the final date)

- remove the enterprise email address from their LinkedIn Profile (ideally on the day of departure)

- transferring the details of any enterprise content that may need to be viewed in the future (copies of emails or InMails, Posts etc)

- removing the person as an Administrator or Manager of any Company Profile, Group, University and change the passwords of individual LinkedIn Profiles accessed on behalf of Senior Personnel

- ensure that the person is signed out of their LinkedIn Profile on any computer or mobile device retained by or returned to the enterprise (see where you are signed in at http://linkedin.com/settings/sessions)

- if relevant, invite the person to join the enterprise Alumni Group

- if relevant, provide details on how the person can continue to support the enterprise as a brand advocate or ambassador in the future and share the details of any reward that is offered for this service

An important point to be aware of is that in a legal sense, if someone is part of your enterprise and they 'get away' with doing something wrong and they are not disciplined at the time of the transgression, it may be difficult to correct this behavior or obtain legal recourse at a later date.

So as an enterprise, you need to think very carefully about what must be monitored. It is much easier to make all of this clear at the beginning of an employment relationship than to try and 'put out a fire' after it has started.

Action 73: *Create an enterprise LinkedIn Social Media Policy based on various items from this book (and perhaps some of your own) and make sure that this is received, read, signed and explained at the beginning of the employment relationship with the individual*

8.6 Effective Strategies For Your LinkedIn Group

There are a number of choices you can make when you set up a LinkedIn Group. The first should be whether or not you have the time, energy and motivation to create a worthwhile Group aligned with your purpose. It takes time to collect members, provide content, encourage involvement and build engagement.

You can create an Open or Closed Group, again, depending on your purpose. It is important to set up a good quality Group Profile (as you did with your LinkedIn Company Page) – including a quality logo, description, links etc and link to the Group on your enterprise website Contact Us page.

Remember to publish your rules and prepare the content for your introduction email when a new member joins. Be ready to personally welcome new members and invite them to contribute. Make sure you always moderate Discussions and invite people to collaborate in other forums outside of the LinkedIn Group.

If your Group becomes very active, you may wish to adjust your settings and only receive daily emails rather than individual emails. If you are part of a large enterprise with many specialties, you may create a number of Groups.

It is a good idea to share the load of managing a Group and not be the only person posting Discussions (but also remember to thank posters both publicly and privately). People who are strong influencers can be invited to post too!

Remember some of the other tips from Company Pages in relation to a Style Guide for Discussions, calls to action, questions etc. You may also like to invite selected people to join the Group via email (from your existing enterprise database – but please don't spam).

Make sure you respond to comments and take action immediately if any inappropriate comments are made. You may also be able to re-use content you have created or collected from elsewhere, provided it is relevant for the Group and you have added a snippet of value to the original piece.

As always, make sure you have proof read any shared content in its entirety before posting it in the Group. Even if you delete content later, people have been known to take screen shots and persecute you in other ways!

Starting Discussions that are slightly more provocative, timely or important can generate renewed energy. But because so many people are so busy nowadays, infrequent quality content is probably far more effective for achieving your purpose than regular, average content.

Action 74: *Be prepared to dedicate time and resources aligned with your purpose if you choose to create a LinkedIn Group*

8.7 Messages From The CEO and Management

The Chief Executive Officer CEO (or equivalent) is usually sourced by the public and the media for comment, particularly in times of crisis. Whilst it would be wonderful to release all information via the enterprise Company Page, the fact remains that journalists, lawyers, competitors and employees will usually want to know something about the leader of the organization (and will look at their personal LinkedIn Profile).

Every leader will eventually leave the enterprise at some point and as an enterprise, you need to prepare for the loss of their influence, reputation, wisdom, knowledge and networks. It is important to have succession plans in place well before their departure, particularly if they have been producing or sharing content via their own LinkedIn Profile as Updates, Posts, Likes, Comments or Shares or authoring Comments on the Company Page or Discussions in the Company Group on behalf of the enterprise.

If the CEO has an extensive network on LinkedIn, this network may actually be more influential and effective than the enterprise's Company Page or Group. But the CEO will need to agree with the enterprise about the content that is essentially shared through their personal network. This will also change when they leave the enterprise.

If the CEO is going to comment on behalf of the enterprise, but also chooses to disclose personal views that conflict with the enterprise purpose, this could be problematic – and this is probably why a lot of enterprises do not encourage CEO's to share enterprise messages through their personal networks (another issue to consider in the Enterprise Social Media Policy).

CEO's often hold other executive positions and this also needs to be factored into the content distribution strategy of the enterprise. Many enterprises are now setting up formal 'Conflict of Interest' procedures and registers to ensure that the relevant governance standards are maintained.

If all of the above is completely transparent and congruent (which would normally be true for individuals in private practice), then the CEO has the ability to complement all of the other online LinkedIn strategies of the enterprise.

Alternatively, the CEO may need to put a disclaimer on their LinkedIn Profile 'All opinions are my own' as often seen on other social media platforms, in particular, Twitter. This could also be an item that is specifically outlined in the enterprise Social Media Policy for anyone in a leadership or management position.

Action 75: *Leaders and managers may need to abide by additional social media policies when sharing content via LinkedIn*

8.8 Getting Sales Via LinkedIn

I know that many people will scan the list of content in this book and head straight for this section!

Let me start by saying that the traditional sales process has changed. In the past, many enterprises relied on printed advertisements in newspapers, flyers and telephone books. Alternatively, prospects were channeled through a sales funnel process – cold prospect, warm prospect, hot prospect, sale, follow up, repeat sale etc.

In my view, the sales model is now based on the idea of exploration, evaluation, sale and if the process is good, further referrals and sales through private networks. LinkedIn describes the process as reach, nurture, acquire. Others describe it as Collect, Connect, Convert or alternatively, Suspect, Prospect, Client.

Selling is a process not an act. People can't 'buy' on LinkedIn, but they can be sourced from LinkedIn and sent to a place to buy. Most experts will say that you don't sell on social media, you sell face to face (or on your own website or in your own store). Others say that traffic is only owned once a person has joined your email list.

Savvy, intelligent and capable people do not want to be sold to (or endlessly pitched to) – they want to find information for themselves – so you need to provide the proverbial 'fish' to catch in the right pool of water!

Up to 85% of business is now secured by referral – so if a consumer hears about a product or service from a reputable source, they will either go straight to the sales step or do some of their own evaluation (due diligence) and then buy.

As so much information is now available in the exploration phase, a lot of people rely on personal referral from someone they know who has expertise in that area.

For example, if I have to make any sort of decision related to information technology, I will never try and source all of the answers myself, I will ask a friend who is an information technology expert. He will usually give me a few clues and tips so I can do some targeted research and evaluate my options a lot more clearly so that I can make an informed choice.

In terms of LinkedIn, in my view, there are three sales goals to achieve the enterprise sales purpose (sales is the generic term I will use for both for profit and not for profit purposes – a not for profit sales purpose could be to get someone to sign a petition, become a member etc).

You need to attract people who are in the exploration phase. You may not necessarily be generating instant sales, it may take time to build the relationship and you will definitely need to remain credible throughout the exploration phase. If you upset a potential client during this phase by pushing a sales message that is beyond their limit, you run the risk of losing them immediately and creating a bad impression that they will share with others. You may not receive an official complaint – but if you investigate a little further, you may find that you have been 'removed' if you are a Connection.

You also need to help people who are in the evaluation phase. You need to make sure that when they look at your online LinkedIn Profile, Company, Group, Posts etc, they can assess and evaluate your content and signals and confirm that they are making the right choice.

Once they have completed the exploration and evaluation phase, you need to make sure that they can quickly and easily move to the sales phase. Please make sure that your purpose can be easily achieved as soon as your potential client lands on your website or visits your store. Don't sabotage your success by failing at this point!

According to Matt Heinz, "Sales is all about being in the right place, at the right time, more often. Luck is a residue of good design. The more generous you are, the more opportunities you can attract. People respond to effort."

I truly believe that social media is a valuable tool to attract clients. It helps you reach specific target audiences, build relationships and generate referrals. If you build your profiles well, you will not only have an excellent digital footprint, you will be able to create a digital asset that constantly generates referrals (although it will still need some maintenance).

By way of example, I met a very smart entrepreneur who has managed to create a Facebook Page with almost one million likes. He has 80 people around the world keeping his content dynamic and generating effective search signals. His sole objective is to collect traffic from Facebook and get them onto his website where he sells a range of merchandise, tickets, products and services of direct interest to his target audience (pop music fans).

Whilst this is working very well for him at the moment, if this was his only online strategy for attracting his target audience, it would be very risky – because the algorithms and rules at Facebook could change at any moment.

As he is making sales on his website, he is also building his enterprise database which, if he keeps them engaged, will allow for continuous referrals and recurring revenue. By sourcing their email address, he then has 'ownership' of the clients (he can't secure this information via Facebook).

The point I am trying to make is that any process you implement to generate sales via LinkedIn should not be exclusively about increasing traffic to your website, it should be about creating conversions – sales. Once that occurs, you need a way to maintain the relationship that suits your client and keeps referrals occurring in the future.

For example, I have been producing monthly email newsletters for Newcomers Network http://newcomersnetwork.com since 2002. That is not too frequent for my subscribers, and most people remain on the mailing list for many years. However, some people have started unsubscribing from email updates now to reduce the number of emails that they receive. I have invited these people who have unsubscribed from my Newcomers Network mailing list to connect with me on LinkedIn – and up to 50% have said yes to the invitation!

This way, I can maintain my relationship with them (just by being active on LinkedIn). Even though I am not sending them a

Sue Ellson

monthly email newsletter anymore, they can still 'hear' my news and be reminded of the value they have received in the past and consider passing on a referral in the future.

What you may have also noticed here is that I am essentially recommending a content marketing strategy that helps build quality relationships that you can follow up with to generate future sales. If you maintain relationships after a sale, you will then secure referrals in the future. Then you will be moving into community management. Think of it as a way to feed forward and generate referrals rather than simply wait for feedback.

There is an old expression in customer service that when someone has a good experience they only tell a few people, but when they have a bad experience, they tell lots of people. You want to keep those good experiences circulating – but if you do get negative feedback, please respond promptly and politely. It is a great tool to help you work out how to do things better in the future!

I will never encourage you to develop a direct bulk message campaign to people on LinkedIn – most people see straight through these sales messages and delete them (and sometimes, they delete their connection with you too).

I am not recommending expensive advertising campaigns either – unless you want to increase your branding rather than make sales as many people notice the 'Sponsored' word and go straight past the information.

I am not recommending that you do whatever it takes to increase your number of LinkedIn Connections either – you need to generate referrals based on relationships and at least seven communication exchanges – not proverbially ask someone to marry you on a first date (as some people expect when they send an unsolicited LinkedIn Connection request and follow it up within 24 hours with a sales message).

I am not encouraging daily posts, updates, shares, comments etc either – you will look like a try hard and most members will either turn off your notifications or remove your Connection as they do not want to be hassled.

LinkedIn is a democratic environment and anyone exhibiting bad behavior will either be detected by sophisticated LinkedIn algorithms or reported by other members – and that does not lead to sales.

I encourage you to play fair and win fair. Add value and you will gain value. Then follow up, make the sale, and maintain the relationship to source further referrals. Remember, givers gain.

Action 76: *Build referral sources over time with an appropriate content marketing strategy that builds quality relationships to secure sales and referrals in the future*

8.9 Follow Up Techniques For Success

Sales staff are often told that if they persisted in their approaches with prospects, beyond the third or fourth contact, they would be much more likely to secure a sale – as a sale usually occurs on the seventh communication exchange!

I always find it fascinating when clients come to me and tell me that they want more new clients, when they already have a comprehensive database of existing clients – and they are not doing anything to maintain the relationship with their existing clients.

Marketing 101 suggests that the best source of new business is from existing clients. So why go through the lengthy process of seven new exchanges to find a new client when a simple follow up exchange with an existing client could be far more productive?

There are multiple ways to follow up with existing clients via LinkedIn. You could also consider some of these techniques to help build rapport with suppliers, stakeholders and shareholders. If you choose any of these techniques, try and make the request as personal as possible. Bulk messages have a very low success rate.

- invite them to Follow your enterprise Company Page

- invite them to Join your enterprise Group

- connect the appropriate employee in the enterprise to them personally

- view their LinkedIn Profile and click on 'View Recent Activity.' Have a look at their recent activity, read the links and Like, Comment or Share (if appropriate and within enterprise Social Media Policy)

- introduce them to someone that may help them with their purpose (via LinkedIn)

- send them a direct personal email and invite them to read a great LinkedIn Pulse Post that is relevant to their purpose

- set up a reminder via LinkedIn to contact them on a regular schedule

- write a Recommendation for them (within enterprise Social Media Policy – and only write what you would say in court)

- endorse one or more of their Skills (if you have witnessed this skill)

- read through their LinkedIn Profile and telephone them for a chat. Mention something from their LinkedIn Profile in the discussion (very few people make telephone calls nowadays, so this personal touch is often appreciated)

- schedule a monthly SMS message and provide them with a personalized message and enclose something useful

- let them know about any upcoming job vacancies at your enterprise in case they know someone who may be suitable

You will notice that all of these suggestions are personal and designed for individuals. Group emails are not well received on LinkedIn as when they are sent via LinkedIn, everyone in the Group receives a copy of each message in that conversation.

I have previously worked with a group of financial advisers and they usually see every client at least once a year. By spending at least 20% of their marketing time on follow ups with existing clients rather than sourcing new clients, they have been able to significantly increase their sales results.

Another extremely important technique is to say THANK YOU. If you receive a referral, always go back to the referrer and say thank you for the referral. After a transaction has been completed, go back and say thank you again and let them know the outcome. If appropriate, you may also like to send a formal acknowledgment – a written card, a small gift etc.

Whilst most of us live in a referral economy, you still need to remember your manners and say thank you! If you receive a referral and it doesn't lead to a sale, still remember to say thank you for the opportunity – that way you may receive another opportunity in the future (and you will be remembered for having good manners).

Finally, one of the biggest mistakes people make in sales is that they ask too quickly and they don't convince the person about the value of the offering up front (usually because they make assumptions about what the person already knows or could be thinking). So don't forget, describe your value, not just your price!

Action 77: *Reconnect with current clients and remember to personally say thank you for every referral even if it does not lead to the outcome you would like*

8.10 Measuring Your Return On Investment

Once again, in the 'good old days' of publishing advertisements in newspapers and magazines, the publication would tell you what their 'circulation' was but they could never guarantee that any of their readers would actually read your advertisement or take action – how could they?

In the digital world, there are a number of metrics you can collect to assess whether or not your time on the LinkedIn Platform is worthwhile.

I believe it is very important for enterprise leaders, managers and employees to understand the concept of 'goodwill.' In enterprise Balance Sheets, on the asset side, a certain value is included as recognition for the ongoing nature of the enterprise.

For example, if the business has 5,000 clients and generates one million dollars in profit each year, it is reasonably likely that the business can continue to generate close to this amount of profit in the following year. Based on a variety of factors, an asset value is calculated around the concept of 'goodwill.'

In my opinion, you can expect to see a new item on Balance Sheets in the future. It will be a 'Digital Asset' amount. This will represent the value of business generated from an enterprise's website, social media profiles, affiliate resources, directory listings etc – anything that is part of the Digital Asset of the enterprise that leads to sales – either without further investment, with maintenance or on a fee for service basis.

For example, if a particular restaurant has secured multiple excellent ratings on a restaurant ratings portal, this may directly lead to multiple referrals to the restaurant and a lot of repeat business. They may have a free listing on Google that doesn't cost anything but with some regular maintenance, the listing helps the restaurant show up in local keyword search results (like Thai Restaurant Suburb Name). They may have paid for a listing on a 'Rewards' type website but this may also generate regular bookings. All of these online 'properties' form part of the asset of the business.

On LinkedIn, there are a number of statistics that an enterprise can collect, monitor and review to measure their Return On Investment:

- number of Company Followers

- number of Group Members

- number of Connections for each employee

- number of Updates sent out via the Company Page or Group

- number of Likes, Comments or Shares on Company Updates

- number of referrals to the enterprise website from LinkedIn (see Google Analytics Data)

- number of referrals generated directly via LinkedIn

- number of jobs you have advertised on LinkedIn (and their results)

- number of ads you have placed on LinkedIn (and their results)

- number of recruits sourced via LinkedIn

- number of emails or InMails received

Personally, you can also track:

- number of Profile Views per 90 days
  http://linkedin.com/wvmx/profile

- number of Connections
  http://linkedin.com/contacts/manage_sources/

- number of Followers
  http://linkedin.com/today/post/author/posts#stats

- how you rank compared to others in your network
  http://linkedin.com/wvmx/profile/rankings

- number of Views, Likes and Comments for each Post
  http://linkedin.com/today/author/77832

- number of Endorsements
  http://linkedin.com/profile/view

- number of Recommendations
  http://linkedin.com/profile/view

It may be a good idea to collect this personal information on a quarterly basis for the CEO or Communications Manager and every six months for your own records. The enterprise may choose their own schedule for data collection. Just remember though that your goal should always be quality over quantity – to build your pipelines, nurture relationships and secure conversions.

LinkedIn also has a range of fee for service marketing products where you can track your spend and results – these are available at https://business.linkedin.com/marketing-solutions – the ads in particular provide very detailed analytics (but you should still be aiming for conversions, not just traffic).

By the way, my recommendation is that you only spend about 20 minutes per week on LinkedIn – unless you are regularly using it for research and follow up.

Action 78: *Decide which metrics you will measure and record them on a regular basis to monitor your return on investment*

8.11 Choose Your Overall Enterprise LinkedIn Strategy

Web developers, marketers and advisers often suggest that enterprises need to constantly create content online to build their brand, reputation and eventually leads. However, there is a lot to be said for considering some of the other enterprise profile building options on LinkedIn like:

- liking, commenting or sharing other people's great content (that you have fully proof read)

- tagging your Connections or saving Followers to your Contacts and giving them a Tag and setting a reminder to follow up with them at some later point

- making sure you include images and/or videos in your Updates to increase your views and conversions (videos generate up to 62% more engagement than pictures)

- saying thank you on a regular basis (one of the most under-utilized free business tools you can use at any time)

It is also a good idea to review and reflect on your performance. I am a firm believer in not reinventing the wheel – so consider finding out what your competitors or inspirers are doing. Monitor the analytics from your Company Updates and see what performs well.

You may like to consider paying for Sponsored Updates (but I wouldn't do this until you had posted at least 50 or more Company Updates and had some analytics to decide what would be worth sponsoring).

Remember that LinkedIn is an amazing research tool and you can also test and try a few things to see what works in your industry and for your clients.

However, I will warn you against non-personalized script style emails or bulk messaging once again – these are probably the least effective ways to build your enterprise on LinkedIn – and you may be penalized by LinkedIn or reported as a spammer. Remember that givers gain!

At the end of the day, completing your Company Profile adequately, participating respectfully and constantly providing value to your target audience will help you build your enterprise profile on LinkedIn.

Action 79: *After testing a range of ideas, create an Enterprise LinkedIn Strategy that will provide value to your target audience and build your digital asset*

9. Generational Tips For LinkedIn Profiles For Individuals

As you travel on your life journey, there are some common trends that you will face going through particular ages and stages. In this section, I would like to provide some general strategic suggestions that may apply when you or someone you know is going through these various time zones. Reacting emotionally can lead to challenges – selecting and implementing good strategies can lead to success.

Action 80: *Understand that on the journey of life, you will go through different phases and you will be more successful if you have a strategy suitable for each stage*

9.1 Students In Secondary Or Tertiary Education

Students are one of the fastest growing segments of people on LinkedIn – it is definitely not a social media platform just for educated professionals!

- include as much detail as you can about your education providers and the subjects you have completed for each qualification (you may also wish to include your date of conferral and certificate number to allow hiring managers to confirm this information if required)

- share information about all of the voluntary work you have completed (even day-long projects)

- describe any Honors or Awards you have received and what they recognized (be specific and provide a link if there is one)

- showcase any involvement in specialist sports, arts, music, student exchange, travel or overseas programs etc

- list your extra-curricular activities (sports, interest groups) in the Interests section

- include rich media that explains your interests for the future

- become a student member of a professional association and include the details on your LinkedIn Profile

- fill in gaps of experience by describing your travel or gap years and what you learnt

- complete the projects section with at least three projects you have completed. Include the title of the project, a description of the project, the challenges you overcame, the results you achieved, the feedback that you received and any future outcomes that occurred (without including any commercially sensitive information – and try using percentages rather than exact figures)

- choose a photo that is aligned with your purpose – not your graduation shot

- mention student as a keyword if you are looking for 'student' positions and would like to come up in these search results (depending on your purpose, you may also wish to include graduate, intern etc as well)

- discuss part time work and all of the transferable skills you have acquired – customer service, supervising, rostering, cash handling, trusted with keys and security codes, abiding by occupational health and safety policies, assisting with inductions

- although you may not have experience in a particular field, if you have studied the topic or have an interest in it, please include these keywords in your LinkedIn Profile – particularly in the Headline and Summary sections

- visit the Student Jobs Portal of LinkedIn at http://linkedin.com/studentjobs

- read Section 10.4 of this book

I encourage students under the age of 18 to review the Teens section in the Safety Center of LinkedIn http://help.linkedin.com/app/safety/answers/detail/a_id/38598 – technically there is no age limit as to when someone can join LinkedIn.

Action 81: *Students have a lot of information they can include on a LinkedIn Profile and I encourage you to become a student member of a professional association related to your future career*

9.2 Early Career

This could be a time when you are working full time, working in casual jobs to supplement your income, still studying part time or combining work and travel. It is an exciting time in many ways as you discover how people achieve results outside of the education environment.

You may find that your digital skills are better than your co-workers, but it is important to remember that you are still in a growth phase and you should see this time as an opportunity to learn as much as you can across a range of disciplines from different people and secure as much real practical experience as you can.

Your goal should be to continue learning, gain as many transferable skills as possible, build up your digital presence and start establishing your networks as a healthy foundation for your future career options.

- keep your LinkedIn Profile up to date with each change in employment

- add more content regularly, remembering to include your primary and secondary keywords

- start building your networks and tagging people into categories

- set up reminders to keep in touch with the new people you meet – do this in a personal manner, not via text

- start publishing some Posts to share your own wisdom

- consider finding a mentor or two and meet with them on a regular basis – offer reverse mentoring if they would like to learn the skills you have

- start attending professional development activities

- get involved with your professional association

- seek out opportunities for further on the job training or education

- ask for feedback from your supervisors and invite them to write a Recommendation for you (also write a Recommendation for them)

- start making connections with people in the industry so that you have an identity in the profession, not just in the workplace

- connect with the people you work with and Like, Comment or Share their content if appropriate

- have a life, interests and hobbies outside of your work

- abide by any Social Media Policy of your employer (and use common sense before publishing anything online)

- remove any inappropriate content you have previously published

Action 82: *Early Career people need to build secure foundations for their future – through training, mentoring, learning transferable skills, building a digital presence and establishing a network.*

9.3 Mid-Career

Mid-Career is a time when you can start to stretch yourself a little more and refine the nature of your work. You may choose to specialize as a technical expert in a particular niche or start moving towards a management, leadership or entrepreneurial role.

You may want to start a side project to really expand your skill set and test your limits. You might be ready for an overseas posting or you may wish to combine work and family or take some time out to raise a family.

You may also be re-evaluating what you want out of life. You may feel as if up until now, you have been living according to everyone else's suggestions – your family, friends, peers, colleagues etc but now, you want to live according to your own values – but, hey, what are they?

This is perfectly normal at this stage of your career – and you need to discover what it is that you value and that usually takes a little longer than five minutes. This is often a good time to speak to a career development practitioner and find out what your options are based on your experience and preferences and you may decide to move in a new direction or modify your existing path.

A general mid-career goal is to keep building and developing your skills, continue learning, expand your digital presence, strategically build your networks and review and reflect on what is important to you moving forward. Make sure you are keeping your values and purposes aligned.

- continue to keep your LinkedIn Profile up to date with each change in employment

- add more content regularly, remembering to include your primary and secondary keywords (these may have changed over time)

- include details of projects and publications

- continue building your networks and tagging people into categories – but also target suitable people to add to your network

- continue to keep in touch with the new people you meet and the people of influence you have chosen to maintain a relationship with

- reflect on your career so far and if you would like to explore some new horizons, start your investigations, source quality information and pursue your goals – take action!

- decide if you need to find new mentors for this next stage of your career and if so, find them

- continue attending professional development activities and offer your assistance

- continue learning and perhaps reading for personal and professional development

- if you haven't already, consider some involvement with your professional association

- look for some unpaid or voluntary work to give something back to your community

- consider flexible unpaid work to maintain your skills and sanity whilst you meet your other commitments (e.g. family, caring for elders)

- ask for feedback from your supervisors and invite them to write a Recommendation for you (and write a Recommendation for them in return)

- continue to Like, Comment or Share quality content that you find – from internal and external sources – build your personal brand in your niche (if you comment on a comment, it goes into the original poster's newsfeed)

- have a life, interests and hobbies outside of your work

- abide by any Social Media Policy of your employer (and use common sense before publishing anything online)

Action 83: *Mid-Career people need to refine their direction for the future – through continuous learning, reflection and review, increasing their brand presence, strategically building networks and taking action*

9.4 Career Changers

It can take a lot of courage to change your career. It could be instigated by circumstance (family, expatriation, retrenchment) or choice, but either way, it can be a significant transition that can either go well or not so well.

Like any challenge in life, a strategy will help. If you have been retrenched or dismissed, remember you are not the first or last person to go through this process. In fact, I can honestly say that being sacked was one of the best things that has ever happened to me – because I would not be doing what I love now if that did not happen!

It is important to be realistic when considering a career change. If you have taken 10 years to build your current skill set and you want to change directions completely, you cannot expect to be equally proficient or equally remunerated by tomorrow. You could find yourself adjusting to a lower income, having a happier life and living in a more authentic manner. A short term sacrifice could lead to long term happiness.

As a way of mitigating some of the risk, I like to encourage career changers to go through this process on a gradual basis. Firstly, I would invite you to fully investigate your dream – all the ins and outs – the study requirements, the market opportunities (looking for specific data and trends) and the realities. If possible, I like to suggest that you get some real life experience in your chosen vocation, to find a mentor in the industry and to speak to other people who are already in the field.

I would also encourage you to look at why you want to change your career. It could be that you are currently working with a boss you hate, but you love the work you do. Is it really necessary to change your entire career? Perhaps you only need to change your employer – or learn better ways to work with your manager?

I am a strong believer in making transitions in stages. A first step is much better than a huge leap. For example, I have seen too many corporate executives go into a franchised business and fail – because they haven't understood how different that type of work is to what they have done in the past.

I have also seen people fall into victim mode. If you didn't want to change careers but you have not been working (either paid or voluntary) for some time, you can start to believe that there is something wrong with you, lose your confidence and start making excuses as to why you can't secure the opportunity you would like.

Once again, it will take a few steps to get you out of this cycle, not a magic pill and a huge leap. If you are in this situation, I would definitely encourage you to start with a small step into voluntary or part time work to gradually rebuild your employability and confidence as you re-adjust to a new way of working.

Another group of people I help are those who have been out of the workforce for some time (by choice) or they are over the age of 45 and they start to believe that they are 'too old' for an opportunity. I believe that it is NEVER too late to work.

You may choose to work in a different way after many years of life experience. You may not want to work 12 hours a day, six days a week, but you might be interested in working 8 hours a day for 3 days a week – using your brains rather than your brawn.

Some later career professionals may have been jet-setting all over the world for 10 – 20 years and the idea of settling down in one location could all be a bit too much. This is when you need to sit down and have a good look at your entire lifestyle – work, family, friends, interests etc and make sure that all of these are congruent – if not, it is unlikely that any job will measure up to your 'past life.'

- continue to keep your LinkedIn Profile up to date with each change in employment and explain gaps in an appropriate way

- add more content regularly, remembering to include your primary and secondary keywords (these may have changed if you wish to go in a new direction)

- include details of your projects and publications and anything else from your life outside of work that is relevant to your future direction

- continue building your networks and tagging people into categories – but also target suitable people to add to your network based on your new direction

- continue to keep in touch with the new people you meet and the people of influence you have chosen to maintain a relationship with

- once you have gathered all the information you need and have had some direct experience in the field, start taking steps towards your new goals

- decide if you need to find new mentors for this next stage of your career and if so, find them

- continue attending professional development activities in your new field

- continue learning and perhaps teaching others

- decide how you will be involved with your professional association

- write Recommendations for others

- have a life, interests and hobbies outside of your work

- continue to Like, Comment or Share quality content that you find – from internal and external sources – build your personal brand in your new direction

- abide by any Social Media Policy of your employer (and use common sense before publishing anything online)

Action 84: *Career Changers need to gather information and experience so that they can make wise decisions, take action over time and move forward with several smaller steps rather than huge leaps to transition to a new career*

9.5 Late Career

I have found that a lot of people in the latter stages of their career either thrive or collapse. This is a time in life when a lot of things start changing – friends and family members often need medical assistance and individuals may need to adjust to a different level of physical or mental capacity.

Children have usually left home and there is an empty nest and a feeling of 'missed opportunity.' If a person suddenly loses their job, it can create a real identity and meaning crisis, particularly if they have been in that role for many years.

Other people who have led a more balanced life, with time out over the years for holidays, friends, families and hobbies often enjoy the change in responsibilities and may look for a role that is relatively straightforward and stress free and pursue some of their other hobbies and interests more frequently.

People who have chosen to be in their own business often find that they relish the opportunity to pass on their knowledge and skills to other entrepreneurs, they take on advisory roles or new initiatives and they continue to thrive on the daily challenge of the business world. In many respects, their enterprise is an extension of their identity.

Whatever path you or someone you know has chosen, now is the time to very carefully align your LinkedIn Profile with your purpose.

- describe your experience in terms of the value you offer (not years of experience)

- continue to learn and attend professional development activities

- share your knowledge through publishing and mentoring

- seek some reverse mentoring opportunities to keep up to date with the latest teachings

- keep your interests alive and your lifestyle congruentmaintain a presence in your profession and keep your finger on the industry pulse

- continue to Like, Comment or Share quality content that you find – from internal and external sources – maintain your personal brand

- keep up your networking and maintain your important business relationships

- source new ideas and keep yourself inspired and motivated

- consider both paid and unpaid work if you choose to change career direction

- be courageous enough to be your true self – be clear on your 'hell yes' and 'hell no' statements that can help people understand your cultural style

- abide by any Social Media Policy of your employer (and use common sense before publishing anything online)

Action 85: *Late Career people have the ability to choose how they perceive their career and their future and remain inspired and motivated by keeping up to date and continually learning*

9.6 Retirement

I have had a range of people tell me that "I don't need LinkedIn anymore, I have retired." I disagree. LinkedIn is a way to keep in touch with people and I plan to keep mine going until I die (then someone else will have to close it!)

Traditional careers have often meant that people have stayed in one job for many years – and for these people, after the initial novelty of retirement wears off, they often find that they miss the friendship and camaraderie of their former colleagues. They may also want to reconnect for personal reasons, but because they do not have a phone number or current email address of the people they have known, they cannot connect. Others start working on their family tree and like finding long lost relatives.

Most people who have a LinkedIn Profile keep their login details current – so it is a good way to 'find' someone many years later. It can also help people see where people have moved over time and how their careers have evolved.

If you are interested in semi-retirement, it can be a way to keep your details 'in the market' and pick up part time or consulting opportunities (or tell people not to contact you if you really want to disconnect). Your purpose can still be adjusted and achieved via LinkedIn – even in retirement!

- be very clear about your purpose

- adjust your headline and summary to indicate when you would like to be contacted

- describe your experience in terms of the value you offer (not years of experience)

- continue to learn and attend professional development activities if you would like to be semi-retired

- keep your interests alive and your lifestyle congruent

- continue to Like, Comment or Share quality content that you find if it is aligned with your purpose

- source new ideas and keep yourself inspired and motivated

- maintain relationships with your key contacts

- abide by any Social Media Policy of your employer (and use common sense before publishing anything online)

Action 86: *Retirees need to be very clear about their purpose and descriptive in their headline and summary*

10. Schools, Colleges And Universities

The Education Section of your LinkedIn Profile is where you record the details of the Education and Training you have completed. If the education provider is well organized, they will have created a 'University' Profile on LinkedIn and you will be able to choose their details from the drop down box as you enter your study details.

A University Profile is essential for any organization that provides training, professional development or education.

Action 87: *If you represent an Educational Facility, please encourage them to have a 'University' Profile on LinkedIn (if they don't already have one)*

10.1 Applying For A University Profile

LinkedIn will not approve every training organization that applies for a University Profile at http://help.linkedin.com/app/ask/path/ up-anup.

The training organization (which may be a professional association if it meets the requirements) needs to be registered with the local authorities and provide quality training that is professionally recognized or accredited to multiple students over many years (not just a Certificate Program).

Before you apply for University Status, it is also a good idea to have created a LinkedIn Company (for all of your staff to be able to list their employment and the public to Follow) and a LinkedIn Group (for discussions).

When you apply for University Status, LinkedIn will check to see how many students have associated themselves with your University (to collect a reasonable amount of alumni data) before approving your request.

Essentially, before you apply, make sure you have collected all of the data that may be useful for approving your University application and include this information in your application. Also make sure that you have a good quality logo, feature image and gallery of photos on your University Profile and a good quality website.

Action 88: *If you represent an Educational Facility, make sure that they have a LinkedIn Company, Group and University Profile*

10.2 Benefits Of A University Profile

A University Profile is a wonderful tool:

- every time a student lists your University on their LinkedIn Profile and chooses it from the drop down box, it shares your branding message and provides a direct link to your University Profile – and then your University website

- it automatically adds the person to your Alumni records

- when people visit http://linkedin.com/edu/, the Universities where they have studied will be listed in the newsfeed

- it enables your University to be on the person's University Selection Board via http://linkedin.com/edu/university-finder

- it enables your University to be on the University Rankings List (mostly US) via http://linkedin.com/edu/rankings/us/undergraduate

- it enables your University to be featured through the Field of Study Explorer via http://linkedin.com/edu/fos

- it encourages the student to connect with other Alumni of the University and see where other graduates are now located http://linkedin.com/edu/alumni

- it enables your University to reach out to your Alumni through LinkedIn

- it allows you to share Updates on your University Profile

- it provides a range of resources for Higher Education Professionals to capitalize on your prospective, current and future relationships with your students at http://university.linkedin.com

Action 89: *Review the range of benefits of having a University Profile and utilize the many tools for your students*

10.3 Tools For Higher Education Professionals

LinkedIn has established a range of tools to help Higher Education Professionals help their students, alumni and parents via http://university.linkedin.com

Tools designed specifically for staff within the university are listed at http://university.linkedin.com/higher-ed-professionals. This section includes an enormous range of videos, tip sheets, presentations, webinars and tutorials.

I believe that it is extremely important for Universities to encourage all of their students, before they leave the university, to update their LinkedIn Profile with the university details and update all of the other sections of their LinkedIn Profile too (I have conducted a range of seminars for universities and secondary schools to help students do this well http://sueellson.com/presentations).

I can assure you that students who have good quality LinkedIn Profiles have a much greater chance of success than those who don't – for a start, they are much more likely to appear in LinkedIn Search Results and interested decision makers have more information to review!

It can also be a tool for University Career Advisers and students who are about to graduate to find out where past students have gone in their career by reviewing Alumni LinkedIn Profiles (and perhaps be a little bold and ask for a referral). Different LinkedIn Groups can be used for specialist subject areas and quality student profiles can also attract employers seeking graduates or interns.

Many students, after completing their studies, do not keep in touch or let the University know the outcomes of their career – but once they are connected to their University via a LinkedIn University Profile, the university can do some research and find out!

It can also be good to help with the ongoing marketing and fundraising for the University. You could invite past alumni back to the school for special occasions, industry updates, research activities or philanthropic donations.

There are a variety of conversations that may also be interesting for you to join or read:

- Career Services Professionals Group http://linkedin.com/groups?gid=2115428

- Alumni and Advancement Professionals Group http://linkedin.com/groups?gid=4173344

- Education Channel (Pulse) http://linkedin.com/channels/education

Don't forget that some of the LinkedIn Tools also give you an opportunity to engage with the parents of students – and these people can be amazing brand advocates and ambassadors or be called upon for industry or profession insight sessions.

How often do you hear parents complaining that they never hear about what is going on at University? If they choose to follow the University, they can hear what is going on and potentially connect with teachers and faculty professionals for further information, particularly if they share a similar passion for a particular topic!

Accounting Departments may also consider reviewing the fee paying capacity of parents (but I would suggest that if they are doing this kind of research, they view LinkedIn Profiles in Private Mode! http://linkedin.com/settings/summary). Some of the tips in this section can be utilized by University professionals responsible for marketing, communications, admissions, alumni and community relations and fundraising, also known as Advancement Professionals http://educateplus.edu.au

Action 90: *Higher Education Professionals have a range of tools in LinkedIn that can help students, staff, parents and the local community*

10.4 Tools For University Students

LinkedIn has created tools specifically for students and these are listed at http://university.linkedin.com/linkedin-for-students

In this section, LinkedIn shares advice on:

- how to build your professional brand

- what to include on your LinkedIn Profile

- how to find a job or internship

- how to go about networking on LinkedIn

- how to tailor your LinkedIn Profile for your goals

The Alumni Tool http://linkedin.com/alumni will help you come up with career ideas and find details of people who may be able to help you find information for your purpose.

LinkedIn also has information about Student Jobs at http://linkedin.com/studentjobs. Visiting this website enables targeted job searches to be automatically created for you. This may not always help you in every location in the world – it requires the hiring organization to classify that they are seeking a student or intern for the role.

As videos are a popular medium with the younger generation (and males), you can also visit the LinkedIn YouTube Channel for more tips and suggestions http://www.youtube.com/user/LinkedIn/videos

---

As a minimum, I would suggest that all students:

- list your post nominals after your name in your Summary section

- if you have secured a professional membership or accreditation, add this to your Certification section

- complete your Education section and choose your University from the drop down box

- if your lecturers and tutors accept connections from students, connect with them throughout your studies (they are often asked by decision makers for the details of good students for unique job opportunities)

- get into the habit of ALWAYS thanking people for referrals, endorsements, recommendations, correspondence etc (I personally do not have time for acknowledging endorsements but I do thank people for the other items listed)

- proof read everything you write on LinkedIn – spelling mistakes are not a good look and negative comments will reflect badly on you – even if you believe they are justified

- respond in a timely manner to every message, notification and connection request (HR managers have a low tolerance for people who do not respond to correspondence quickly and they don't want to message you on Facebook just to get a response)

- remember that if you have a well completed LinkedIn Profile and your fellow students do not, you have a better chance of coming up in LinkedIn Search Results

- specifically read Section 9.1 in this book and review the rest of this book to learn how to achieve your purpose with LinkedIn

Action 91: *LinkedIn has a range of tools specifically designed for students – review these if you are a student, alumni or parent to help you achieve your purpose on LinkedIn*

10.5 Add To Profile Qualification Or Certification Button

LinkedIn has created a quick and easy tool to help students add a completed qualification to their LinkedIn Profile from a direct piece of University correspondence.

To create this 'Add to Profile' feature for a Degree for your University, simply visit http://addtoprofile.linkedin.com and follow the instructions.

To create an 'Add to Profile' feature for a Certification, simply visit http://addtoprofile.linkedin.com/cert and follow the instructions.

Action 92: *Universities can help their student graduates add a qualification or a certification to their LinkedIn Profile via http://addtoprofile.linkedin.com*

11. International Purposes

For some years now, experts have been talking about a 'global war for talent.' Governments have developed programs to attract leading thought leaders to their major cities to attract the associated talent, kudos and international exposure. Individuals have started mapping out careers based on where they would like to live next. Expatriates no longer fall into the stereotype of a white male who can speak French with an accompanying stay at home wife.

Some enterprises still haven't grasped the concept of international labor and are locked into the idea of sourcing candidates that are already based in their location. Other organisations have tried to outsource significant components of their operations to countries with a cheaper labor force and have saved money in the short term but have often lost business in the long term as a result of miscommunication and cultural differences.

Personally, I would like to see every enterprise combine a healthy mix of both international and local talent of all abilities in their workforce and operate with a much greater level of social responsibility and engagement with their local community. Well managed diversity in a labor force has consistently been shown to generate good results.

The relative ease of travel, visas and the broader use of English in the business world has also enabled many more individuals to obtain long term and short term international work experience. However, the main reason for expatriate assignment failure has always been related to the unsuccessful adjustment of the accompanying partner or family to life in the new location.

Fortunately, with the increase in communication technology, it has become easier to remain connected to a home location (Skype, emails, online news, specialty food stores etc). It has also become easier to consider yourself for international opportunities through LinkedIn.

Let's explore some of the ways you can achieve an international purpose with LinkedIn:

- you could change your location to the location where you want to go – this will help you come up in that location's search results – but in the address box in the Contact Info section, please explain where you are based now and when you plan to arrive in the other location (remember, you must never lie)

- start connecting with people in your 'future' location – you may choose to do this by letting your existing network know that you are interested in roles in Italy for example. You could then ask them for any referrals to people they know in that region (not just that country)

- reach out to people in the new location that have previously worked in your location – they will know what it is like to move to that location and may be more willing to provide suggestions

- follow some target companies where you would like to work

- start liking, commenting and sharing content related to your purpose that has been produced by people in your industry or profession in that region

- reach out to selected individuals and see if you can organize a live online chat (say via Skype) and have some questions ready for your discussion (but limit the first call to a maximum of 10 minutes – you don't want to come across as demanding)

- review LinkedIn Profiles of other locals in a role similar to what you would like – observe how they have told their story, what recent activity they have completed and the type of content they share

- connect with local career advisers and recruiters and try to understand how the recruitment process works in the new location (it could be very different to your current location and you may need to re-write your resume, CV or LinkedIn Profile to suit local market demands). Consider paying for professional assistance to speed up the process of securing work and understanding the local work culture once you find a job

- improve your cultural intelligence – you really need to find out as much as you can about the new location before you arrive. Consider paying for some relocation assistance (for finding somewhere suitable to live) and cultural training – a modest fee up front can save you a huge amount of time, money and embarrassment on arrival. Make sure that when you do move, you have someone to meet you at the airport when you arrive (a good first impression makes a significant difference to your overall success in a new location)

- be prepared for challenges. If you expect it to be challenging, you will adjust much more quickly. Put in place new routines and rituals to create a sense of home and purpose. Find trusted local mentors and new friends as quickly as possible

- understand that you are going to go through a transition period when you move to a new location. In your old location, you were probably unconsciously competent with most aspects of your life. Now you will need to re-learn a lot of your automatic behaviors (even simple things like washing the dishes) and this takes a lot of extra time and energy – so go easy on yourself

- remember that if you choose to repatriate to your home location or move to another location, the whole process will start again – if you are strategic in your approach and you have learnt from your mistakes, you will potentially adjust a lot quicker. If you don't apply a strategy and if you react emotionally, you could find yourself facing unnecessary challenges

Action 93: *There are several ways to attract and discover international opportunities through LinkedIn – but please consider paying for professional career, relocation and cultural advice if you are moving to another location*

12. Personal Branding And Reputation Management

"Just build your brand from day one, man. Your brand is your name, basically. A lot of people don't know that they need to build their brand, your brand is what keeps you moving." Meek Mill

There are some very simple suggestions for developing and maintaining a good brand and reputation on LinkedIn. Some people do not like the idea of a person being a 'brand' – but as I have mentioned in this book – so many opportunities occur via a referral and when an interested party wishes to verify that referral, they will most likely complete an internet search and your digital 'brand' (your name) will appear – particularly if you have a LinkedIn Profile.

Your reputation will be revealed by the activity you complete. If you are generous and share good quality content that is useful for your target audience, this will help create a good reputation – particularly if you provide it on a consistent basis (good quality information at least three times a year is a good start).

Branding is also about being truthful, following up, doing what you say you will, remembering important dates, using your manners and being punctual. But remember, at the end of the day, you can only control the controllable.

Action 94: *Your digital brand can be showcased via LinkedIn and your reputation can be developed by sharing good quality content on a regular basis*

12.1 Personal Branding Tips

Personal Branding is about creating an ongoing impression about what you do and how you do it. It is implicated in your 'hell yes' or 'hell no' statements on your LinkedIn Profile but it is also more clearly defined by the computer experience, user experience and the strategy and tactics you use on LinkedIn (see Section 3.3, 3.4 and 3.5).

There are some other tips and techniques I can suggest to improve your personal brand on LinkedIn.

- **be authentic** – people can see through false statements and will quickly disengage from your broadcasts if they are not authentic, particularly if you are constantly trying to sell a product or service

- **be considerate** – focus on solutions rather than criticism. For example, you can include controversial content in a Post, but you need to make suggestions on ways forward rather than condemn existing practices

- **be collaborative** – encourage sharing of good quality content – even if it is in your area of expertise. Computer algorithms like to see like content with like content – so supporting others can be good for your search results

- **be generous** – say thank you to everyone who comments on your content and provide further specific feedback or acknowledgement

- **be punctual** – it seems that most people are busy nowadays – but timely responses are always well received

- **be courageous but polite** – it never hurts to ask for information (it can hurt to ask for an immediate sale) but you do need to be respectful and courteous. If there is a way that you can provide help first before asking, do so

- **do not expect free referrals or professional assistance** – just because they have a free LinkedIn Profile doesn't mean they want to help you for free

- **be willing to assist** – whilst you may not be able to provide direct assistance to someone, if you can refer them to someone else, you will be remembered favorably

- **follow up** – I cannot over emphasize this point – ALWAYS say thank you and make an effort to follow up after interactions with valued connections and clients

- **be accountable** – if you do make a mistake along the way, be willing to apologize and make amends if possible. Never ridicule another person in the process

- **seek professional advice** – if you are in a high level position, you may need to be trained to handle a crisis, the media, social media, law enforcement agencies, governance and compliance issues etc

- **don't make assumptions** – this is an easy trap – find out what you need to know in any given situation and respond appropriately rather than react emotionally. If you cannot respond instantly, let people know that you are investigating the issue and will respond as soon as possible (and make sure that you do respond)

- **be proactive** – there will always be new features and options on the LinkedIn Platform so make an effort to keep up to date and utilize these benefits for your purpose

Action 95: *Consider how your behavior on LinkedIn will affect your personal brand and choose techniques that will help you achieve your purpose*

12.2 Reputation Management Tips

In days gone by, large newspaper publishers could virtually destroy a person's reputation with one story and the public would virtually remember the incident forevermore (because everyone was reading the same content).

Nowadays, with the proliferation of published information, a 'huge story' can virtually appear and disappear within hours (as mentioned earlier, if you can survive the first 18 hours, you will probably be fine).

It is possible to successfully manage an online reputation and I have shared a number of ways to increase the size of your digital footprint so that you can reduce the risk of negative content appearing at the top of Google Search Results.

However, that is simply a risk mitigation strategy rather than an increased opportunity strategy.

To help influence and control your reputation, you need to decide what you are going to publish, where you are going to publish it and what associations you are willing to develop (both with people and online platforms).

In terms of associations, you can consider whether or not you would like to be a part of LinkedIn and whether or not you will connect or not connect with certain people. You may also choose not to be a part of certain online platforms (like Facebook http://facebook.com or Pinterest http://pinterest.com) if it is not aligned with your purpose (or the amount of time you have available to maintain your activity levels on the platforms to make them worthwhile).

Let's look at a specific example. I was working with a very senior executive head hunter and he has an extensive array of connections in one political party (right up to the Prime Minister level). He also has a personal interest in horse racing and is on a first name basis with many high profile celebrities.

The nature of his work means that he has to be very careful about who can see his Connections on LinkedIn (you can change the setting so that Only You can see your Connections but shared Connections will still be visible http://linkedin.com/settings/summary), how much information he can publicly disclose (about himself or his clients) and what description he uses for the work that he completes.

He conducts most of his business by intimate personal telephone discussion, so he is far better off making direct contact with individuals by telephone to maintain his business relationships – but he could use LinkedIn to quickly find their contact details and keep a cloud based and personally updated 'black book' of their details! In his case, he doesn't need Facebook, Pinterest, Instagram etc but he can definitely utilize LinkedIn to remain visible to his clients.

Depending on your purpose, you can choose to manage your reputation by:

- fostering strategic personal or business alliances through LinkedIn

- creating or participating in relevant LinkedIn Groups

- following particular Companies

- completing a regular Update or Post schedule for yourself or your enterprise

- following a particular Style Guide for all of your published content

- maintaining a certain level of online activity to keep your reputation current

- continuously learning and growing and sharing your insights along the way

- completing additional qualifications and certifications and showcasing these in your LinkedIn Profile

- sourcing complementary external resources to enhance your reputation (like an ongoing Google Search Results Program, an Online Reviews Gathering Strategy or publishing Recommendations and Testimonials on your website)

- selectively responding in an appropriate manner to content aligned with your purpose in your LinkedIn newsfeed, Group Discussions or Company Updates

Reputation Management is also about perception. How do you want to be perceived online? If you are 'always' online and always posting, commenting, sharing etc, you may be perceived as having too much time on your hands and not really working at all.

If you do not participate in any activity at all online, you may be perceived as a dinosaur and not part of the current online world.

This is why it is again important for you to think about your purpose. It may be more appropriate for you to participate in a niche industry forum rather than

LinkedIn if your reputation needs to be fostered in that environment rather than the more general LinkedIn environment.

I am always a little reluctant about putting all of my 'eggs in one basket.' I believe a modest LinkedIn Profile is a minimum requirement for everyone.

Action 96: *Consider which techniques you will use to manage your reputation online. Be selective when choosing which platforms to use and always act in alignment with your purpose*

12.3 Networks You Need In Your Life

For a successful life, I believe that you need to secure and maintain three types of networks in your life.

A personal network – made up of your friends and family.

A professional network – made up of the people you work with in your professional life and the other people in the wider industry or profession.

A social network – where you enjoy a hobby, sport or interest and can connect with people outside of your family and work networks.

If you can establish these three networks in your life and one network becomes less effective at a particular point in time (for example, when you are suddenly retrenched and your work network is weakened temporarily), your other two networks can help sustain you and give you the support and encouragement you need to keep on going.

A network is also a place where value is shared – both given and received – so you may notice that if you are not giving, at some point you will probably notice that you are not receiving either.

I often see people who do not create a solid professional network. You need to develop a wider network than your immediate employer or enterprise because the world changes very frequently and this network can:

- keep you up to date with changes

- provide you with professional development opportunities

- share new ideas and inspire you

- challenge you and keep you moving forward

- provide support if needed

Each of the three networks requires some level of contribution, maintenance and development. You cannot expect to always receive – there are quite often unwritten rights and responsibilities – so it is always worth adding in a little more and taking a little less and finding out from people in your field the nuances of these networks in the local area so that you can maximize your opportunities.

If at some point your personal brand or reputation is challenged via LinkedIn or any other online content, simply remember that at some point, it will pass and you will move on. Your networks can often provide the genuine support you will need.

However, during a crisis period, regardless of the circumstances, I encourage you to be as respectful and as polite as possible, even if another person is behaving unethically.

Action 97: *There are various ways to manage your brand and reputation online and if you develop personal, work and social networks in your life, you will have additional support available if a challenge occurs*

13. Research

"Research is creating new knowledge." Neil Armstrong

You may have already tried a general search from the box on the top of your screen in LinkedIn – but this is just the most basic search you can do on LinkedIn. Right next to this box, it says 'Advanced Search' http://linkedin.com/vsearch/f?adv=true and to the left of the box, you can choose whether you would like to search People, Jobs, Companies, Groups, Universities, Posts or your Inbox. Interestingly, you can also do searches via Google and if you have optimized your content on LinkedIn, you have a chance of having your LinkedIn content appear on the first page of Google Search Results.

You may also be using LinkedIn for other research too. Did you know that search engines still have 300% more traffic than social media? Social media is a good place to do some social homework before buying (or selling). A lot of people 'discover' what they need or want on social media.

Action 98: *You can complete general and specific searches within LinkedIn and via Google and if you optimize your LinkedIn Content, you can also make it perform in Google Search Results*

13.1 Searching For People

Naturally searching for people is a regular task completed by recruiters, head hunters, human resource professionals and business owners, whether they are looking for potential candidates or verifying the details of a particular candidate.

There are a variety of search fields that you can choose to find someone, but personally, I have found the keywords and the location boxes the most helpful. Remember that you can also use Boolean Characters in search fields (things like ? for a single character, * for several characters, "" for must include etc).

Your search results will usually be skewed towards your first or second level connections (another part of your purpose strategy) and once you have completed a certain number of searches, you will reach a 'commercial use limit' (which is why I sometimes combine searches on LinkedIn and Google) that will be re-set each month.

When you meet this limit, your search results will be limited to the top four pieces of information for your query. If you would like unlimited searches, you will need to upgrade to one of the LinkedIn Business Plus, Sales Navigator or Recruiter products.

A search result is only as good as the content in the database and although many people have a LinkedIn Profile, many people do not tell the full story in their LinkedIn Profile (which is why I encourage you to put as much information as possible related to your purpose in your LinkedIn content).

If you have a Premium Account, your LinkedIn Profile, if it is similar to another person's profile, will appear higher up in search results (promised as twice as prominent). You will have access to a more comprehensive range of search criteria (Groups, Years of Experience, Function, Seniority Level, Interested In, Company Size, When Joined) and be able to reach people directly with an InMail message.

Action 99: *Be smart with your searches on LinkedIn and remember that if you want to come up in search results, you need to include your primary and secondary keywords in your LinkedIn content*

13.2 Saving Your Searches

When you create a search on LinkedIn http://linkedin.com/vsearch/f?, on the top right hand side of your screen, you can choose to Save search. This will enable you to repeat your search on a regular basis and you can also set an alert for the search to run automatically every week or month (and then view the results).

Premium LinkedIn Products http://linkedin.com/premium/products allow more Saved Searches and this may be helpful for people who are in a sales, marketing or business development role.

These Saved Searches enable you to look for content listed in LinkedIn Profiles as well as content in Companies, Groups, Posts etc. So if you have a particular interest in a specific niche, this could be a great way to receive this targeted content.

Action 100: *Consider setting a Save search for information you would like found automatically every week or month*

13.3 Taking Action From Your Searches

There are many LinkedIn Trainers and Experts around the world who provide various processes, scripts and systems for creating leads or sales via searches you have conducted through LinkedIn.

Remember that throughout this book, I have encouraged you to take ethical action based on your purpose – so if you are willing to consider any of these offers, please make sure that they are authentically aligned.

Also remember that the LinkedIn algorithms have been created to detect bad behavior and individuals can easily report spam. You must abide by the LinkedIn User Agreement.

My personal belief is that if you really want to reach individuals, LinkedIn is a great tool to find the person – and if you contact them seeking or providing information in the first instance (rather than demanding a sale), you have a much better chance of generating multiple exchanges that will eventually lead to the conversion you are seeking.

Once you have created a communication exchange, don't give up after the first message. Following up and persisting over time (roughly seven exchanges) is much more likely to generate a conversion. LinkedIn has tools to help you in the 'Relationship' tab – where you can Tag people, make Notes, set Reminders and describe How you met.

Please don't limit yourself to People searches. Accessing information from Companies, Groups and especially Posts can be extremely helpful and can enable you to increase your ability to share useful information around the LinkedIn Platform.

Action 101: *Take authentic and persistent action after finding content via a LinkedIn Search*

14. Referrals

As I have mentioned previously, up to 85% of business is generated through referrals and the best new employees are usually referrals from existing employees or their families and friends.

It makes sense that to source a referral, you can start by considering the people you already know – and LinkedIn is a huge international network that you can search on demand at any time. You can decide to focus on people within your network or outside of your network. You can also find an individual who may be able to lead you more directly to the right person (asking questions is usually an excellent way of reaching the right person a lot quicker).

For example, I could have met a person at a networking event and catalogued them in my own mind as being an information technology (IT) professional. On any given day, I could be looking for a specialist in a particular aspect of IT for either my own needs or the needs of one of my clients.

By completing a search on LinkedIn, I could find either a person or a company that offers this skill set. For an individual, LinkedIn will tell me how we are connected, when we connected, what messages we have sent to each other via LinkedIn and show me any other information I have added in the Relationship tab. I can then drill down and review this information and the information in their LinkedIn Profile (including their Recommendations) and reach out as required.

The reality is that I am unlikely to remember the details of all of my Connections (thousands of people), so this LinkedIn Search functionality allows me to find referrals within my network (or outside my network if I choose to do so).

Action 102: *Remember to search through your network on LinkedIn when you need a referral as you may not always remember the details of everyone you are connected to either as an individual or as a company*

14.1 Referral Marketing

To trigger referral marketing for either a job or an enterprise, you need to establish a presence that enables people and companies to find you when their need arises. If they know you and remember you as an expert in a particular area (because your behavior online keeps them informed about your capabilities), then you have a much greater chance of them coming to you when they need your expertise or recommending you when they meet someone else who needs your expertise.

So like many other aspects of business, there is no single magic bullet that generates referral marketing. Good marketing is not an expense, it is an investment based on persistency and consistency. You need to have a strategy that keeps your presence alive in the market so that you are the first person who comes up in either someone's thoughts or search results. Ideally, they will see you as a subject matter expert, the go-to person, trusted authority, key expert or thought leader. You don't need to say that you are any of these people, you simply prove it with your actions.

Your search results will be enhanced by improving the Computer Experience (Section 3.3). Your branding and reputation can be enhanced by continually sharing good quality content (provide the BEST content, not BULK content) and behaving authentically. Your conversions will be increased with clarity, appropriate calls to action and persistence. Bad content comes across as 'noise.'

There are some additional ways that you can also generate leads or referrals:

- you can stay one step ahead of your competitors by utilizing new tools effectively (like adding good quality video content or infographics)

- don't try and start from scratch all the time – rely on existing relationships and ask for referrals rather than start out with a cold call to someone who has never heard of you

- provide content that can easily verify your credibility (lists of publications or books, recommendations, reputable connections in your area of expertise)

- be the nice guy who celebrates success and achievement with a short note of congratulations when good news appears rather than the person who is always selling a particular message

- always be prepared to review what works and what doesn't work and ask yourself questions about your analytics and your results and confirm whether or not you are achieving your goals as you may need to change your approach

- don't be too pushy or salesy – referral business is generated by pulling people in not pushing yourself onto them

- make promises and keep them and even consider under promising and over delivering (for example, you could say that you will complete a task by Friday at the latest but if you deliver it early than promised on the Wednesday before Friday, you will have 'over-delivered')

- assume that it is a long term strategy and that it will take time – but don't be complacent and just wait around, take small steps regularly

- focus on good quality referral sources rather than a huge quantity of referral sources – a good lead can be 'almost sold' when they arrive and a bad lead can be a waste of time

Action 103: *Referral Marketing is a longer term pull strategy and if you carefully build good quality referral sources, your purpose can be almost achieved by the time the lead is referred to you*

14.2 Referral Sharing

For many years now, I have had a policy of not accepting affiliate marketing invitations for either online or personal referral systems that essentially enable me to profit from providing a referral. I have found that in most cases, these programs have been a vehicle for the other enterprise to receive free advertising and I have received either no reward or very little reward for the promotion I have provided. That is not to say that these programs cannot work, it has just been my experience that they have not been either profitable or helpful.

On the other hand, I can happily report that I regularly refer my clients and friends to people using LinkedIn. I mostly refer people that have approached me for goods and services that are outside of my current priorities and I willingly pass on their details to people I know (with disclaimers and specific suggestions just in case!). Because

I have a large network, I am also asked – "Do you know someone who does X?" Naturally, I provide referrals in this case as well.

Unfortunately, I have been disappointed that on most occasions, the people receiving the referral do not say thank you or provide any feedback on the outcome of the referral (when I specifically tell the person who has received the referral to mention my name when they contact the person or enterprise).

I make a personal effort to thank everyone who sends a referral my way and I also like to let them know how things turned out in the end (without revealing any private information).

Thankfully, this approach has often lead to more referrals.

I also make an effort to acknowledge anyone who has given me more than one referral and I try to provide them with some sort of tangible benefit (like some free LinkedIn Consulting Advice, a direct referral to some potential work or a personal career or business strategy implementation session).

If you wish to use LinkedIn to gain referrals, for a job or enterprise, you also need to think about how you will use LinkedIn to give referrals. You will need to decide whether or not you will ask for a referral fee (these are quite common in some countries but definitely not customary in Australia and in some cases, particular industries are regulated and referral commissions need to be documented – for example, in real estate).

Action 104: *Decide how you will refer people or enterprises to others and remember that if you are wanting to receive referrals, you also need to give referrals*

14.3 Referral Automation

More and more individuals, freelancers and enterprises are looking at ways to automatically generate referrals through LinkedIn. I have already mentioned that by being clear on your purpose, selecting the right computer experience and user experience and employing the right strategy and tactics, you can achieve your purpose, which is essentially making sure that you have created a digital asset that generates the conversions you want.

LinkedIn has been quite protective about allowing developers to connect into the LinkedIn Platform via an application programming interface key (API key). The information you have personally provided in your LinkedIn content enables LinkedIn to provide all sorts of in-house auxiliary premium products – and if this intellectual property was accessed through another platform, they are at risk of losing their major asset.

Successful businesses make acquisitions on their journey (as LinkedIn has) and they also grow organically (by adding additional features and benefits on a regular but measured basis). To my knowledge, there are no specific direct products that work directly with the LinkedIn Platform to automate referrals, but I do recommend that every individual or enterprise establish methodical procedures so that when you up-scale your lead generation and referral efforts, you do not lose any of your past efforts along the way.

For example, if you are part of an enterprise that has a sales team, individual sales people may connect to potential customers, but it should also be a part of the Social Media Policy and practices that these prospects are added to the enterprise database as essentially, they have been 'paid for' by the enterprise (not the individual sales person working for the enterprise). The enterprise Customer Relationship Management System (CRM) should be able to track the prospect throughout its lifecycle, but also identify the origin of that lead – LinkedIn.

An additional level of automation can be acquired through the personal efforts of a paid employee, freelancer, consultant or virtual assistant. I do not recommend that they fill in personally created spreadsheets as these have so many limitations and most people do not understand how important it is with any data to have each piece of information in a separate field (for example an address should be separated into multiple fields including a street address, a suburb, a country, a state/region and a postal/zip code). It is also important for each individual or enterprise to only have one source of truth (or one database).

A standard procedure for an enterprise would be to encourage anyone associated with the enterprise to Follow the Company on LinkedIn (not always easy to do as most people like to connect with people, not Companies).

I do recommend that enterprises use well recognized Mailing List and CRM platforms (like MailChimp http://mailchimp.com and Salesforce http://salesforce.com) as these popular programs are more likely to be able to develop integrations with other popular use programs in the future (even if the initial cost is a little higher than platforms offering similar features).

Because of their popularity, if LinkedIn does allow some level of connectivity or integration in the future, it is more likely to consider the popular programs as integration partners well before the non-popular programs (where you may need to export your data and then import it into another compatible or non-compatible system and then face the additional costs of data migration).

Action 105: *Develop practical systems to manage your referral gathering process now and in the future in preparation for any future automation program*

15. Relationships

How many times have you heard that people like to work with people they know, like and trust? That people you meet go from being a stranger to a friend over time and if you manage this process well in the business world, they can morph into a companion (regularly liking your content), a crusader (sharing your content, a brand advocate (regularly providing referrals) or ambassador (representing you and sourcing direct referrals).

Content is a very good way to build trust and a relationship. At the end of the day, people do business with people (not just brands).

Other types of relationships have developed on LinkedIn too. Long lost childhood sweethearts have re-connected across continents. Long lost relatives have been added to family trees (genealogy). Previous partners, friends, work and professional colleagues have searched for you online to determine what you are up to now.

Action 106: *Developing relationships via LinkedIn can help create advocates and ambassadors for you or your brand and reconnect you with people from your past*

15.1 Building And Developing Relationships

What I appreciate about LinkedIn is the ability to have my personal and business address book accessible from any internet enabled device. I also value:

- the automatic visibility generated through my Updates and Posts

- the notifications emailed directly to LinkedIn connections

- the notifications that are sent directly via the Notifications icon (for example, "Sue Ellson has published a new Post…")

- the analytical data showing search sources and view totals

- the ability to find someone when I can't remember all of their details but I do a search via keywords and manage to find them

- the opportunity to find someone's current email address or phone number directly (if they are connected to me)

- the ability to source guest speakers or individual people in an enterprise when I don't know the actual name of this person

- the options for tagging connections to sort my personal database

- the quality of the digital footprint it creates for me personally, my businesses and the content I write in Pulse

- the surprises it generates by helping me appear in LinkedIn Search Results

All of these features help build and develop quality relationships and a majority of these functions are automatic, provided I contribute a certain amount of content and remain active on LinkedIn.

There is no way that it would be physically possible for me to do all of these activities on my own. The LinkedIn Platform also generates both LinkedIn and Google leads whilst it maintains and develops my relationships.

Action 107: *Remember that the LinkedIn Platform automatically builds and develops your relationships through a variety of automatic processes*

15.2 Changing And Challenging Relationships

Due to the automatic nature of some activities on LinkedIn, I have personally chosen to disconnect from some people on LinkedIn. I have chosen to do this because I don't want the processes of LinkedIn to remind them that I exist.

Some of my clients have removed Connections because of bad work or personal relationships or because the person has died and the LinkedIn Profile has not been closed by the executor.

You can remove a Connection by searching for them and then when you visit their LinkedIn Profile, next to the blue drop down box in the middle of your screen, you can choose to Remove and/or Block them.

Alternatively, you may wish to remain connected to the person but you may not want to see their Updates in your newsfeed (perhaps because they are sent too frequently and are not relevant to your purpose). In the top right hand side of their Update in your Newsfeed, there is a down arrow. When you click on this arrow, you can either choose not to see the content or Unfollow the person.

Regardless of the reasons why you wish to disconnect or stop viewing information from another person or company on LinkedIn, I do recommend that you be polite and respectful at all times. If you are concerned about your personal safety, please discuss this with reputable local welfare authorities or the police.

One of the best ways to stop unwanted attention, as I have told many of my clients, is to stop thinking about that person, worrying about the issue and responding to any messages. These clients have often protested intensely when I have suggested this action – but I can assure you that this technique has been very successful. Focus your time and energy on your purpose, not theirs.

If the LinkedIn Platform is being used inappropriately, you can report this to the LinkedIn Safety Center where your concern will be investigated. This center has a range of other very useful tips and suggestions for staying safe online, keeping your account secure and it also explains how to use LinkedIn successfully http://help.linkedin.com/app/safety/home.

Action 108: *Visit the LinkedIn Safety Center to review various tips and techniques about safety, security and privacy and how to use LinkedIn successfully*

15.3 Relationships That Have Ended

Unfortunately I have also had to assist family members who have lost a loved one and on one particular occasion, it was a woman's nephew and he had been tragically killed in a car accident. She asked me how to access his LinkedIn Profile so that she could let his friends know the details of his funeral. She was not sure whether his laptop was accessible or not but apparently she did have access to his email address (probably via his mobile phone).

Naturally, this is a very distressing time for a family member and for security reasons, LinkedIn cannot automatically grant any person access to the deceased person's LinkedIn Profile.

This is why it is so important for you to create a list of all of the usernames and passwords you have for:

- every online account you have ever had

- your email addresses

- your social media profiles

- your government and health records etc

- your utilities and services

It is a good idea to have columns in your Usernames and Passwords Spreadsheet (available FREE as an Excel Spreadsheet download when you join our 120 Ways Publishing Membership Program http://120ways.com/members) for:

- the category for the item (business, personal, membership)

- the date the account was created

- the name of the account

- a description of the account

- the URL link to the account

- the email address you used for the account

- the username or number for the account

- the password for the account

- your membership number or details (if you have one)

- any other details necessary to access the account

- the details of any additional security questions you needed to answer

This Usernames and Passwords Spreadsheet should be kept electronically for your own use but also printed (with the location of the digital file included in the print out) and put with your Will or important papers so that at the time of your death, the allocated person can close all of your accounts. (I do not rely on Password

Programs because if your computer or phone dies, you lose access to all of your accounts).

For people who are worried about security, please remember that someone else with access to the emails on your phone could quite easily re-issue your passwords. If you have trusted your passwords to someone else (like a virtual assistant) and you decide to terminate their service, having a list like this makes it very easy to login to all of your accounts and quickly change all of your passwords (even better if this is done before their dismissal).

The only accounts that I would include on the list but not record a password next to would be your financial accounts (banks, shares etc) – that way your cash assets will only be released to the beneficiaries in your Will after probate has been finalized.

So for the Aunty who lost her nephew, as she did not know the password for his LinkedIn Profile but she did have access to his email address, she could have the password reissued and then login and download a list of all of his Connections.

Assuming he had less than 2,000 Connections, she could then import these details into a new MailChimp http://mailchimp.com account and for free, send out individual emails to all of his Connections.

If she tried to message his Connections via LinkedIn, she would only be able to message 50 people at a time and every one of those 50 people would be identifiable in the message and if just one person responded to that email, it would automatically send that message to the other 49 people that received the first email (very inappropriate in this situation).

His Executor has to decide what to ultimately do with his LinkedIn Profile (I would suggest that it is a good idea to always make a LinkedIn Profile 'not visible' to the public as soon as possible via http://linkedin.com/profile/public-profile-settings).

It may have been necessary to transfer administration rights for Companies or Groups to other people, to share details of certain Connections with other enterprise partners or to Save a copy of the LinkedIn Profile for use in the eulogy and to give a copy of his

LinkedIn Profile to selected family members and friends. Ultimately, the LinkedIn Account should be closed (visit http://linkedin.com/settings/summary and choose 'Account' and then 'Close your account').

Unfortunately here in Melbourne, a much loved member of a local Professional Association had a LinkedIn Profile that was left online for several years after her untimely death.

This meant that her Connections continued to receive automatic Notifications directly via LinkedIn – for example, suggesting that they congratulate her for her work anniversary or birthday etc. LinkedIn were not to know that she had died, but these automatic Notifications were very distressing for the recipients. The account has now been closed.

This is also the reason why our society now has 'Digital Executors.' People who close the dormant accounts of deceased individuals. The beneficiaries can waste a lot of money paying someone to track down and close accounts when they don't have a Usernames and Passwords List to start with – so I really do encourage you to make your own Usernames and Passwords List as soon as possible. It has the added benefit of saving you time entering all of your obscure passwords because you can simply copy and paste your password when you login to your accounts.

Finally, on the issue of Passwords, I recommend that you choose different passwords for all of your accounts. If this is too complicated for you and you want to be able to login anywhere without a Usernames and Passwords List, you may like to create a password formula.

You could include three capital letters, three lower case letters, three numbers and three symbols (this format should comply with most password systems) and preferably choose characters that don't look like another number or letter – like a small 'l' and the number '1'. When you login to LinkedIn, you could replace the third letter with an 'L'

ACLxtr634+*%

When you login to Google, you could replace the third letter with a 'G'

ACGxtr634+*%

When you login to Facebook, you could replace the third letter with an 'F'

ACFxtr634+*%

Naturally if you have two accounts that start with the same letter, you could add in a second letter. So for Facebook, it might change to

ACFAxtr634+*%

All you need to do is remember one sequence and then apply your formula to the item you are logging in to. It is not a foolproof system, but it is a whole lot better than using the same password for multiple accounts!!

Action 109: *To have a record of all of your online accounts, create a Usernames and Passwords List as soon as possible and print out this list and put it with your important documents in preparation for the day when all of your accounts need to be closed*

16. Achieving Your Goals

"Discipline is the bridge between goals and accomplishment." Jim Rohn

You probably already know that to achieve your goals, you need to:

- write them down

- work out ways to achieve them

- take action

- get help if required

- overcome challenges

- remain persistent

- be patient

- celebrate your successes

- acknowledge those who have helped you and always say thank you

- review your goals and your performance

- start again with new goals

Once you are clear on your purpose, and you have generated the relevant computer and user experience and you have implemented the right strategies and techniques, it won't be long before you realize that you are actually starting to achieve your goals. This clarity will also enable you to leverage the full power of LinkedIn as you will be able to focus on what works for YOU.

Action 110: *Once you have defined and achieved your goals, you need to review your performance and start again with new goals*

16.1 Top 20 Tips And Techniques

Most people like to think that there is a shortcut to success – a quicker and easier way to secure some 'quick wins' and generate an immediate result.

The only time that a shortcut appears before a success is in the dictionary!

If you don't have the time or the inclination to complete most of the suggested actions in this book, I encourage you to start with the following top 20 tips and techniques.

1. Decide on your purpose and stick to it

2. Select your primary and secondary keywords and put them in your LinkedIn profile in the most important positions – Headline, Current Job Title, Past Job Title, Education, Summary, Experience

3. Complete as many sections as possible in your LinkedIn Profile, Company Profile or Group and be reasonably active

4. Always proof read everything you publish, like, comment or share before pressing Save or Send

5. Create a Style Guide for your purpose so that your behavior is always consistent and is search engine optimized for your purpose

6. Stay up to date with the various features and functions of LinkedIn (visit and click around at least every six months) and incorporate the best features for your purpose

7. Be strategic when you source new Connections, Followers and Group Members and determine which VIPs you will personally keep in touch with more frequently

8. Decide on what you will measure and how often you will record this information so that you can accurately assess whether or not you are achieving your purpose

9. Regularly review your viewers, your responses, the leads, the conversions, the analytics, the notifications to source clues as to how you can increase your performance

10. Understand the nature of the platform and its power as a network builder, content publisher and research tool and use these features to your advantage

11. Access the relevant Apps, Jobs, Influencers, Channels, Newsfeeds (Personal, Company, Groups) for your purpose

12. Consider the Premium LinkedIn Products – but only after you have fully maximized all of the Freemium Options and have enough results from your various efforts to truly gain the value from the Premium Products http://linkedin.com/premium/products

13. Understand the nature of business and the value of integrating your offline and online networking, referrals, thank you's and follow ups. Make a habit of connecting to every new person you meet related to your purpose on LinkedIn and think about introducing people you know to other people in your network on a semi-regular basis

14. Adapt your processes to the various life stages you go through but also the different purposes that are related to either jobs or enterprises. Source solutions rather justifications

15. Understand other people if you are in the job market (HR managers, recruiters etc) and your target audience (if you are part of an enterprise) and remember that this is not just about you, it is also about them

16. Don't let anecdotes or limiting beliefs stop you from achieving your purpose, but be realistic about the choices you make and take action based on factual evidence, faith and persistence

17. Remember that you are now part of an international market and this can give you both opportunities and challenges. Remember that you need to constantly learn and grow to remain relevant to current market conditions

18. Measure what is relevant, review this information and make choices about what you will do next to achieve your purpose

19. Relax a little but also have a range of risk mitigation strategies in place to manage your branding and reputation, even if you are a very private person. If you are in an enterprise, make sure your colleagues understand and comply with the enterprise's Social Media Policy

20. Ask and pay for professional help if you need assistance with writing, keeping up activity levels, producing and/or sharing content or understanding the tools you need to use for your purpose – and to be most effective, consider establishing an ongoing review process from an expert (or join the 120 Ways Publishing Membership Program http://120ways.com/members)

Action 111: *Review the top 20 Tips and Techniques and make an effort to complete at least one of these in the next month*

16.2 Your Minimum Targets

I am often asked what are the minimum targets that you should be aiming for through LinkedIn – so here are my suggestions:

- collect a minimum of 60 Connections

- aim to have 100 or more views per 90 days

- publish 6 or more recommendations (you may have to ask for them)

- secure 20 or more endorsements for your top 10 skills

- login to LinkedIn for a minimum of five minutes per week

- record your number of views for the last 90 days, save your profile to PDF and export your Connections at least once every three months

- update your LinkedIn Profile and add in any new content in new fields at least once every six months

- if you have a Company Profile, share an Update at least once a month

- if you run a Group, generate a good quality discussion at least once a month

- create and publish three good quality Posts per year

- Like, Comment or Share an Update in your Newsfeed at least once a month

- connect to an average of one new person or more per week

- write three or more Recommendations per year

- endorse at least one person per month for selected Skills

- make an effort to meet face to face or speak with one of your Connections every month

- congratulate at least one person every month (for a job promotion, good Post, sharing good information)

- personally thank every person who sends you a direct referral

- respond to any direct messages you receive via LinkedIn as soon as possible (and preferably within 24 hours)

- process your Connection requests once a week

However, I will include a disclaimer here. If these targets are not within your purpose range, ignore them! You may need to choose different targets or higher targets – only you can choose the best options for your purpose.

Action 112: *Select some minimum targets you would like to achieve with LinkedIn and go for it*

16.3 Questions And Answers

Whilst I have covered a lot of different topics in this book, there are some very common questions I receive and I have summarized a small selection here. I have also spent a lot of time compiling the Index in the back of the book so please consider looking for individual items there.

1. Who should I connect to or not connect to on LinkedIn?

This will always depend on your purpose. If you want to build a large network, you may be a bit more flexible and agree to more invitations and source more new Connections. If you want to specialize in a niche area, you may be highly selective. I encourage you to visit every person's LinkedIn Profile before you accept a connection request and make an assessment as to whether or not they match your purpose or if they are a spammer. Remember that you need to connect for a purpose, not for sport – it is not just a game!

If you personalize a connection request, you are around 50% more likely to receive an acceptance – so please avoid sending bulk invitations via email or clicking 'Connect' from the 'Who You May Know' screen.

2. Should I connect to my competitors on LinkedIn?

Again, it will depend on your purpose. LinkedIn algorithms will favor LinkedIn Profiles that have similar content and connections but from a personal perspective, you may feel threatened by the LinkedIn connection and be worried about the competitor approaching your connections for business or sales (you could change your Connections visibility to 'Only You' but shared connections will still be visible).

You can decline an invitation (and it does not personally notify the person that you have declined) – but when they look at their Invitations Sent http://linkedin.com/people/invites they will be able to see that the Invitation is outstanding and has not been accepted. If you do decline the Invitation, it will stop LinkedIn from sending reminders about the Invitation request.

Also remember that not every person likes every other person – so even if the competitor is connected to one of your Connections, it doesn't mean that your Connection will leave you and go to the competitor (especially if you have superior products and services).

3. What should I include or not include on my LinkedIn Profile?

Again, it will depend on your purpose. Some people worry that too much information will be overwhelming to viewers – but remember, you need to attract the right viewers to your LinkedIn Profile first (via keywords and activity) and in this respect, the more content the better.

That said, you do not want the User Experience to be a bad one. If your content is complex, inconsistent, difficult to read etc, this will be off putting. Make sure that it is logical and relevant for your purpose.

You can include capital letters in your content, but not in titles or too frequently as this is classified as 'shouting' in the online world. I often use capitals as a way of putting in a heading in the Description box in the Experience section of my LinkedIn Profile (DESCRIPTION, TASKS, ACHIEVEMENTS, CONTACT etc)

It is absolutely vital for you to make your purpose clear and enable viewers to take the next step. LinkedIn is an excellent referral tool. If you are not clear, the viewer will not take action.

4. When should I update my LinkedIn Profile?

I would suggest fairly regularly (at least every six months) – but especially when there has been a change in your Experience section, you have completed a Project or Publication that you wish to add to your LinkedIn Profile or a new feature has been added to the LinkedIn Platform (as completed LinkedIn Profiles are up to 40 times more likely to appear in search results).

5. What items should I Like, Comment or Share?

Again, it will depend on your purpose. But you absolutely must read any links in full and you must also comply with any enterprise Social Media Policy or guidelines. Liking and Commenting adds a good statistic to the originator's Update, Post or Discussion, but Sharing really helps the message go viral (so absolutely make sure it is okay to share first).

If you Share someone else's content, they will be notified and they are likely to be grateful. If someone shares your content, I would encourage you to personally say thank you for sharing the content.

6. When should I share an Update (or Publish a Post)?

Various analysts will tell you that there are better times of the day and better days of the week that are more suitable for sharing your content. If you work in an international industry, you may also need to think about the time zone of the majority of your target audience. I tend to avoid Fridays and the weekends, but again, this all depends on your purpose (and in this case, the nature of the content).

7. What can I write in a Post and can I republish something I have already written?

In my view, the best Posts provide useful information and they do it in an interesting and engaging manner. They are not full of sales pitches and they are easy to read with an excellent layout and no spelling mistakes! They may include some additional media (image, video, infographic etc) and they can be either long or short – but if the headline gets me in and the content is awful, I will always think twice about viewing content from the same person in the future.

Yes, you can republish content you have written elsewhere (provided that it is within the terms of the first publisher's arrangement). For example, some news websites insist on exclusive content that is not published elsewhere.

Google does not like Duplicate Content. If their robots see that the same content has been published twice, they will add the first appearance of the content to the Google Search Index and ignore the second instance. They do not mind if you publish content on somewhere like LinkedIn first and then on your own personal website, but they certainly do not want you to write one article and publish the same content (even if it is slightly modified) on 20 other websites.

8. Where is the best place to use LinkedIn for maximum effect (phone, tablet, laptop, computer)?

This is a challenging question. I personally prefer to use LinkedIn on my laptop or computer because I can see the full range of features and access all of them (whereas I cannot do this on a phone or tablet with the internet browser as LinkedIn will only provide the mobile version of the LinkedIn Platform on these devices).

However, LinkedIn has created various apps and some of these apps are very convenient to use on the run on a phone or tablet – so if these apps help you use LinkedIn when you otherwise wouldn't, they are a great benefit. Also, some of the apps have features that are not available via an internet browser.

9. How much time should I spend on LinkedIn?

Again, it will depend on your purpose. I login almost every day as LinkedIn is one of the main tools I use to generate business and maintain relationships.

However, I would never encourage anyone, even the best sales representatives, to spend more than an hour per day – you need to focus your activities on what works for your purpose (don't be distracted by all of the 'weapons of mass distraction' out there!). As a general rule, once your LinkedIn Profile is fully completed, you could probably average 20 minutes per week and allow a little additional time for completing other tasks if you are either looking for work or sourcing business via LinkedIn.

I spend most of my social media time on four major social media platforms (LinkedIn, Facebook, Twitter and Google+) and I have chosen these four because they are the most relevant for my purpose. I know LinkedIn the best and I believe I have sourced the most opportunities through LinkedIn, so I also spend the majority of my time on this platform.

But as I have already said, I never put all of my eggs in one basket and one of the most vital platforms for me is my personal and enterprise websites (where I can fully control the content). A multichannel social media approach will also help you avoid the risk associated with algorithm changes (for example – notifications originally went to all LinkedIn Connections, now they go to a limited selection).

If you really want to think about whether you should or shouldn't do something, even though I abhor anything to do with gambling, ask yourself "Would I bet on this working?" How much would you be willing to bet? $1 or $100? Could you guarantee that by completing that task, you will win and get the outcome you desire? This can be a quick way to really identify how relevant you believe the activity will be in relation to your purpose.

In some cases, I do believe you should 'pay to play.' If there is a tangible benefit in a premium product of service, don't expect it for free, pay for it and really get some value! Especially if there is a fair exchange. For example – if you put in $10 and you make $100 then you have benefited – why would you bother trying to save $10?. Do you really expect a free lunch all the time?

10. I prefer to meet people face to face and not communicate online – why do I need to be on LinkedIn?

No person must be on LinkedIn just because Sue Ellson recommends it! Like many other people, I have found it extremely helpful and I have been able to achieve various purposes through LinkedIn. I have built a large international network of Connections and been able to automatically maintain these personal and professional relationships. I have sourced business and job opportunities and referrals, received recognition and congratulations, found guest speakers, have completed research and due diligence and been well educated through a variety of updates and content.

LinkedIn's most significant benefit to me is that it has enabled me to do all of these activities far more efficiently online than I could ever do in person. It has the potential to take me away from face to face networking, so that is why I make a particular effort to go to live events and meet people in real life.

As a general rule, I find that the people who worry about communicating online or having an online presence are usually worried because they don't know how to do it and no-one has explained it clearly or appropriately for their needs.

So again, think about your purpose. If you are an artist, living as a hermit in a forest and you have a steady stream of people paying you appropriately for your artwork, you are well connected in your local community, you have other interests, you can easily keep in touch with your family and friends and you do all of this without an online presence and this is the way you want to live your life, I would suggest you don't need LinkedIn!

11. Why do I have to have a LinkedIn Profile when I already have other online profiles?

I have one client who is an Author and she has a profile on Goodreads http://goodreads.com – and she wants to keep a very low personal profile online and just sell books through her publisher. She sees LinkedIn as a business platform rather than a personal platform. I have encouraged her to keep her LinkedIn Profile for a little longer as it is highly search engine optimized (her Goodreads Profile comes up on page 2 of Google Search Results but I know that if she made her LinkedIn Profile visible, it would come up on page 1 of Google Search Results). For now, her LinkedIn Profile is visible to no-one (and this matches her current purpose). So if you are in a similar situation, you could do the same.

For most people, LinkedIn is their own 'little black address book' keeping them in contact with both their professional and personal network. Even after retirement, it is a way to reach out to former Connections. In my view, I would be more inclined to delete other online profiles and keep a LinkedIn Profile (which is what I did when I deleted my Xing http://xing.com profile as I am not concentrating on doing business in Germany).

12. What about privacy?

As mentioned earlier, LinkedIn has a comprehensive Safety Center http://help.linkedin.com/app/safety that provides information about Privacy http://help.linkedin.com/app/safety/answers/detail/a_id/38595

I only provide information that I am happy to have in the public domain and I have a very clear message so I do not attract unwanted attention. I also avoid releasing information about where I will be at a certain time (unless it is for a public event).

13. How do I measure my return on investment (ROI)?

There are various ways to measure your return on investment – and that is why it is so important to be clear about your purpose. Increasing the number of views to your LinkedIn Profile or Company is pointless if it doesn't lead to the outcomes you desire – remember, clarity leads to conversion. There are two sections in the book that talk about ROI (Sections 2.6 and 8.8).

14. What other online platforms do you recommend for people wanting to increase their Digital Footprint?

As a minimum, Google+ http://plus.google.com. Next, as a general rule, Facebook http://facebook.com and Twitter http://twitter.com as they have such a large share of the current market.

There are special platforms for certain purposes – like Meetup http://meetup.com for finding local events and Instagram http://instagram.com if you have a lot of visual content. You really need to think about your purpose before deciding which platforms to join. I have experimented with a wide range and if they don't deliver in terms of performance, I close my account and move on.

15. Do I have to put a photo on my LinkedIn Profile?

No. However, LinkedIn Profiles with photos are seven times more likely to be viewed (according to LinkedIn). Now I do understand that some people are particularly shy or private so I always recommend that you choose a photo that you are comfortable sharing (and it should be a professional style photo related to your purpose rather than a party style photo with other people in it).

One of my clients has a very stylish photo with her sunglasses on – but it is still her and it fits with her purpose! If you don't include a photo, ask yourself why? Are you serious about LinkedIn, or just curious?

16. How much information do I need to include on my LinkedIn Profile and how far should I go back in time?

This topic is discussed in Section 6.6. I recommend that you include all of your history, but you should still align it with your purpose. I have chosen to highlight some aspects in my past and remove others as they are no longer related to my purpose (but I never ever lie). I include enough information so that I appear in LinkedIn Search Results and I write it in such a way that it still makes sense (it is not just Search Engine Optimized text).

If you are looking for work, what would your ideal employer expect? The truth, the whole truth and nothing but the truth? Or an edited version? Does it add more keywords to your profile? Does it show your ability to move and grow throughout your career? Can you focus on explaining the most appropriate skills rather than duties like 'cleaning the office kitchen?'

As a recruitment specialist, I like to understand the whole person. If you are worried that your 'age' is an issue, then you may need to remember that if the employer discriminates on age, you might get an interview but not the job. What you can do though is demonstrate how you can add value to an organisation (skills, knowledge and networks), not just skills.

Remember, many older workers are classified as loyal, reliable (no childcare issues) and hard-working and may be exactly what the business seeks.

Describe yourself in terms of the value that you bring rather than your years of experience (most people use years of experience to give you an 'old' label).

For example, a 22 year old recruiter is unlikely to comprehend the value of 25 years of experience...but if they can see that you have a huge range of skills in the area they are recruiting for, the process is simple – and they will probably think you are a guru!

17. How often should I Post on LinkedIn?

I would not recommend more frequently than once a month – and it needs to be good quality content – but that said, if you have a lot to say as a writer, and it is beneficial for your purpose, you may wish to publish more frequently.

18. Should I pay for Premium LinkedIn Products?

In the first instance, I believe that you should update all of your LinkedIn content and activity and make sure it is all fully aligned with your purpose. You are actually helping LinkedIn by providing this content as it makes their database and published information more useful and they can on-sell various products (so don't feel guilty about having a Freemium account).

However, there are many benefits to having a Premium Account:

- you will appear higher in search results

- you can complete more searches

- you will have better analytical data (seeing all viewers for the last 90 days and more details about the referral sources)

- you will have some 'prestige' value as the Premium Status is featured on your LinkedIn Profile

- you will have the ability to message people directly via InMail

If you are in an enterprise, there are various solutions to help you with marketing, recruitment, lead generation etc

Disclaimer: These benefits may change in the future.

So, like all Membership Programs, you need to review what is on offer and maximize the free options first. When you are ready to either have a one month free trial or a personal visit from a LinkedIn sales team member, make sure you are ready to take action and maximize your new opportunities with systems and processes that you can implement from day one (even if you have to pay someone to show you how to make these things work for your purpose).

19. How can I reduce the number of emails in my Inbox from LinkedIn?

You can go to your Communications Settings from your Privacy and Settings at http://linkedin.com/settings/summary and adjust the frequency of emails you receive.

It is also a good idea to set up a rule on your email Inbox and ask your email program to send every email from "@linkedin.com" to a particular folder and that way, you can check all of the emails from LinkedIn in the one location. You simply need to remember to look in that folder on a regular basis.

20. Should I write my LinkedIn Profile in the first person or the third person?

I discuss this in Section 3.4 – Firstly, I would avoid the anonymous 'no' person' because it sounds too impersonal.

Whether you choose the first person or the third person depends a little on your purpose. Australians do not like people who boast and if a profile reads 'I, I, I, I' over and over again, we find it over the top. If you choose to use the first person, try not to use 'I' more than three times in the summary section.

On the other hand, if you refer to 'Sue, Sue, Sue, Sue' over and over again, that looks bad too.

When you read text, it is much easier to read about 'Sue' which is about me, rather than read about 'I' but comprehend that you are reading about Sue. When I see the word 'I' it makes me think about me, not you. For example, which is easier to understand?

'I have optimized and improved many LinkedIn profiles'

or

'Sue Ellson has optimized and improved many LinkedIn profiles.'

In the first instance you were thinking about Sue but reading the word 'I' which is actually you.

In the second instance, you were reading about Sue and reading the word 'Sue.' This could be easier for your brain to interpret.

Conversely, as people know that you have written the content, if you use the third person, that can be seen as a little bit 'removed' whereas the first person could be perceived as more personal.

It all depends again on purpose. For example, if you were a really out there creative artist, 'I' may be more appropriate. If you are a CEO of a Fortune 500 company, you may wish to have content that is 'ready for publication' in a biography.

I prefer the third person, but I have also recommended the first person in some cases. First person can appear like you are talking directly to the reader, can build more trust and be more relatable and social. Third person can appear slightly removed but it can be better for search engine optimization because you will be repeating your own name more often. You will need to choose what is right for you.

Action 113: *Asking questions is a great way to find the answers you need – and you can also find answers by looking in the Index of this book*

17. LinkedIn Special Features

LinkedIn has a range of special information, products, resources and apps that you can access directly via a website link listed in this section (or your phone or tablet App Store) and sometimes via the footer menu on certain pages when you are logged in to LinkedIn.

Action 114: *LinkedIn has a variety of special information, products, resources and apps that you can access via the LinkedIn website or your phone or tablet App Store*

17.1 LinkedIn Information

LinkedIn has a variety of information that is not always immediately obvious from the screen when you login – so I encourage you to check out some of this information.

- **about** http://ourstory.linkedin.com provides a historical infographic. More information is at http://linkedin.com/about-us and the page I find most useful is at http://press.linkedin.com/about-linkedin

- **investor** relations http://investors.linkedin.com provides information to shareholders. It also provides links to information about the LinkedIn enterprise and management team. You may be personally interested in the LinkedIn Annual Reports http://investors.linkedin.com/annuals.cfm

- **newsroom** http://press.linkedin.com provides details of LinkedIn Press Releases and various resources and links useful for journalists. Some of the links from this subdomain are listed below

- **lists** http://lists.linkedin.com is where LinkedIn compiles interesting reports based on the performance of individuals and companies

- **brand** resources http://brand.linkedin.com provides information on the branding guidelines for LinkedIn logos and how they can be reproduced on any digital or printed materials. You can also download original files

- **security** http://security.linkedin.com provides information on security for members and customers and it links to the Security Center http://help.linkedin.com/app/safety/ home that provides practical tips on how to stay safe online for adults, teens, parents and educators. Information that can be shared with law enforcement agencies is also discussed. If you have a concern that you wish to report, visit http://help.linkedin.com/app/safety/answers/ detail/a_id/146

- **help** http://help.linkedin.com the help center is very comprehensive and provides answers to a lot of popular topics. There is a help forum where you can post a discussion (and respond to others). If you want to contact LinkedIn directly (and you have already searched the help center and couldn't find an answer), you can contact LinkedIn directly via a 'ticket' system at http://help. linkedin.com/app/ask. LinkedIn also has some 'learning webinars' at http://help.linkedin.com/app/answers/ detail/a_id/530

- **help requests** http://help.linkedin.com/app/account/ history provides a list of all of the help requests you have made

- **we heard you** http://members.linkedin.com/we-heard-you provides a list of the most-requested feature updates and fixes LinkedIn has recently completed

Action 115: *LinkedIn has information about their history, investment performance and branding available online. The newsroom has a range of information suitable for journalists and the safety and help centers are also useful for further information*

17.2 LinkedIn Products

As mentioned previously in Section 2.9, LinkedIn provides a range of Premium Products that can be accessed via http://premium. linkedin.com and http://linkedin.com/premium/products

- These products are designed for both individuals and enterprises.**premium products** – where you can upgrade

your account to access more features and data http://
linkedin.com/premium/products

- http://premium.linkedin.com/jobsearch Job Seeker –
  find work

- http://premium.linkedin.com/professional Professional
  / Business Plus – expand your network

- http://premium.linkedin.com/premiumhiring Premium
  Hiring / Recruiter Lite – find and recruit talent

- http://premium.linkedin.com/sales Sales Navigator –
  social selling

- **small business services** – where you can market, brand
  and sell through LinkedIn http://smallbusiness.linkedin.
  com

- **business solutions** – where you can market and sell
  your business offerings – Talent Solution products for
  recruiting, hiring and employer branding http://business.
  linkedin.com/talentsolutions

  - http://business.linkedin.com/talent-solutions/recruiter
    Recruiter – find talent

  - http://business.linkedin.com/talent-solutions/recruiter-
    lite Recruiter Lite – find talent (but less often)

  - http://business.linkedin.com/talent-solutions/
    advertise-jobs Job Slots – advertise jobs

  - http://business.linkedin.com/talent-solutions/post-jobs
    Job Posts – advertise jobs

  - http://business.linkedin.com/talent-solutions/job-
    adsWork With Us Ads – puts job ads directly on
    people's LinkedIn Profiles

  - http://business.linkedin.com/talent-solutions/
    company-career-pages Career Pages – social media hub
    for employer branding

- **sales solutions** – where you can prospect and sell by
  keeping in touch with various targeted individuals and

companies via social selling (selling based on building relationships)

- http://business.linkedin.com/sales-solutions

- http://business.linkedin.com/sales-solutions/products/ sales-navigator

- Sales Navigator for individuals or teams

- http://business.linkedin.com/sales-solutions/financial-servicesSales Solutions for Financial Services

- **marketing solutions** – helping you to reach people directly (even if you are not connected)

  - http://business.linkedin.com/marketing-solutions

  - http://business.linkedin.com/ marketing-solutions/ products/lead-nurturing Lead Accelerator – nurture prospects through targeted ads

  - http://business.linkedin.com/marketing-solutions/ products/native-advertising Sponsored Updates – puts ads within updates

  - http://business.linkedin.com/marketing-solutions/ products/sponsored-inmail Sponsored InMail – send emails direct to people

  - http://business.linkedin.com/marketing-solutions/ products/display advertising Display Advertising – puts ads online

As mentioned throughout this book, I encourage you to maximize the free options first as these will help prepare you for the premium products available through LinkedIn. An effective online strategy requires a good foundation.

LinkedIn Sales Staff are also available in many international locations to provide extra training and support for a variety of these solutions.

Action 116: *Once you have maximized the free services of LinkedIn, consider the Premium Products on offer*

17.3 LinkedIn Resources

- **Blog** – the official LinkedIn Blog is like enterprise blogs that are sorted by topics, recent and popular posts http://blog.linkedin.com

- **Talent Blog** – is another LinkedIn Blog that specializes on topics related to talent, careers, recruitment etc http://business.linkedin.com/talent-solutions/blog/topics

- **Elevate** – allows employees to start sharing company updates through their personal networks http://business.linkedin.com/elevate (this is a paid feature)

- **Referrals** – encourages employees to provide referrals to new employees http://business.linkedin.com/talent-solutions/employee-referrals (this is a paid feature)

- **Developers** – where you can integrate LinkedIn features with your other online initiatives – probably most useful for the people helping you with your website and data integrations http://developer.linkedin.com

- **Engineering** – provides details of how LinkedIn engineers work with their data sets and open source projects and how they support women in technology. It also has a blog and jobs section http://engineering.linkedin.com

- **Economic Graph Challenge** – LinkedIn is interested in developing the world's first economic graph and has opened the project to the wider community. Read and participate via http://specialedition.linkedin.com

- **Certified Marketing Partners** – if you need extra help with the LinkedIn products and services, LinkedIn can direct you to relevant partners http://business.linkedin.com/marketing-solutions/certified-marketing-partners

Don't forget that most website designers can also add a variety of plugins to your enterprise website and enable your website visitors to share content via LinkedIn, share a newsfeed etc

Action 117: *LinkedIn has an official blog where you can find announcements. They also have information for developers and their engineering section goes into more detail about how LinkedIn works with their data sets. If you are interested, consider getting involved with the Economic Graph Challenge*

17.4 LinkedIn Apps

LinkedIn has developed and retired a variety of Apps and the App features are constantly changing – so I would like to suggest that if you are interested in using LinkedIn via your mobile device, you add these Apps to your phone or tablet and have a play!

Some of the features offered by the Apps are not available on the desktop version of LinkedIn. Likewise, some of the editing and publishing options on the desktop version of LinkedIn are not available via a LinkedIn App.

- apps – these are listed at http://linkedin.com/mobile with links to both the Apple Store and Google Play and include:
    - LinkedIn for Phone – mobile apps
    - Job Search – find a job
    - Pulse – tailored news
    - Groups – chat with others in groups
    - SlideShare – view presentations, infographics and video
    - Lynda – learn new skills
    - Lookup – find, learn about, and contact co-workers
    - Recruiter – find and respond to talent on the go (paid)
    - Sales Navigator – find and engage with the right prospects (paid
    - Elevate – build your reputation by sharing smart content (paid)

Action 118: *LinkedIn has a range of Apps that you can use on your mobile devices – just remember that some features are only available via Apps and some features are only available via the Desktop version of LinkedIn*

17.5 LinkedIn Tools

- **Opportunity** http://opportunity.linkedin.com shares stories about how other people have utilized LinkedIn and provides you with an opportunity to share your personal story with LinkedIn

- **Non Profits** http://nonprofits.linkedin.com provides a huge range of options for organizations seeking volunteers. There are sections for finding employees, finding board members and social fund raising. It also leads you to the LinkedIn for Good Program which showcases the pro bono work completed by LinkedIn and how to apply for grants from LinkedIn. Their grants system focuses on opportunities for youth and veterans

- **Pro Finder** http://linkedin.com/profinder has been developed to help freelancers and professionals connect to opportunities (a bit like a trade listing to help attract opportunities) and if you are interested, you can register at http://linkedin.com/profinder/pros. It can also be used if you are looking for a freelancer or professional – just list your project at http://linkedin.com/profinder/projects

Action 119: *LinkedIn has a range of special tools for attracting opportunities, getting involved in the non-profit sector and for helping freelancers and professionals connect with projects*

17.6 LinkedIn Indexes

LinkedIn has developed two indexes that compile your data and performance to produce a report that helps you understand your results in a different way.

As always, make sure you use a range of information from different sources before making important personal or business decisions.

- **Social Selling Index** http://business.linkedin.com/sales-solutions/social-selling/the-social-selling-index measures your personal performance in relation to how you have completed your LinkedIn Profile, how you find people, how you engage with the content on LinkedIn and how you connect and establish trust with other LinkedIn Members.
  You can click on a button and get your score for free.
  It is updated daily and gives you a score out of 100 and measures how you compare with other people in your industry and your network on LinkedIn (don't forget that this is something you may wish to record on a regular basis, particularly if you are in sales)

- **Talent Brand Index** http://business.linkedin.com/talent-solutions/products/talent-brand-index this is a tool that has been designed to measure an enterprise's talent brand in the marketplace. It is available on request from LinkedIn and would be very relevant for larger organizations that regularly recruit new staff via LinkedIn

Action 120: *Consider using the LinkedIn Indexes to understand your results in a different way*

18. Future Of LinkedIn

"The future belongs to those who prepare for it today." Malcolm X

Like any social media platform or technology, if you review how much the platform has changed from its inception, you can definitely confirm or deny whether or not it will last by the way it has evolved and adapted over time.

The original premise of LinkedIn – creating a network for professionals – remains today. It is just the way that your network is built and developed through LinkedIn has changed. You can now incorporate the value of Posts, Groups, Companies, Tags, Reminders, Advertisements, Apps and more.

There has also been a variety of system changes over time. I remember when the Skills and Endorsements Section first appeared and there was a huge outcry because so many false endorsements were being recorded and sales people were using these false votes as a way of sweet talking connections.

I admire LinkedIn for persisting with this feature, even though they faced a huge backlash in the beginning. It often takes guts to make a decision and stick with it and as this particular feature does not significantly impact your personal LinkedIn Search Results, but still offers value to the reader of your LinkedIn Profile, it was a wise decision.

LinkedIn has also experimented with various system features like Events (which shut down in 2012) and Apps (like Connected in 2016). There have also been various types of Personal Membership, Talent Solutions and Sponsored Advertisements products and packages.

Naturally, to remain financially viable, LinkedIn has chosen a range of income streams to spread their risk. (Someone once told me that most millionaires have at least seven income streams).

They have also been clever about protecting their Intellectual Property by only allowing plain text data entry (to reduce hacking attacks) and limited downloads of contact information for all of your connections (only first name, last name, email address, current job title and company name for each connection).

Based on this information and my own thoughts (and perhaps my perfect wish list), I would like LinkedIn to consider the following options in the future:

- a premium service that allows integration with an enterprise CRM (like Salesforce http://salesforce.com)

- an alternative CRM platform that operates through LinkedIn (like the external service Nimble http://nimble.com that amalgamates information across social media platforms but also integrates with an in-house system like Salesforce)

- a messaging system that allows people to see when you are online and start an online chat immediately (like Facebook Messenger) that is available via a desktop computer (not just an App)

- a comprehensive site map that links to all of the LinkedIn resources and subdomains mentioned in this book (I wish!)

- additional training to encourage members to complete more of their LinkedIn Profile so that the database asset value can increase further (perhaps including suggestions from this book)

- more targeted campaigns to acquire members across different work sectors (not just professionals but also students, graduates, semi-skilled, semi-retired and retired)

- more acquisitions of related technologies or platforms (like MailChimp for emailing but with a premium service)

- continued expansion into additional countries (as they have done with China and incorporating WeChat http://wechat.com as the local majority social media)

- more B2B functionality to improve the ability for business to business transactions to be conducted exclusively through trusted networks of LinkedIn

- increased cyber security and spammer security to protect the integrity of the platform

- enhanced use of the big data collected from the platform to identify key influencers in certain markets and ways for LinkedIn Staff to connect personally with these people (for example, providing local Master Classes and Exclusive Networking Opportunities for these LinkedIn Brand Advocates and Ambassadors)

- more content in different formats – for example, you can already see videos playing in the Newsfeed (as happens on Facebook), but I predict that there will be other publishing formats (not just SlideShare) that will be incorporated in the future (podcasts, eBooks, interactive apps available online through the internet browser and not just via a phone download) and perhaps integration with live video streaming (like Periscope http://periscope.tv)

- developers are well known for attempting bigger and better things than their counterparts at similar organisations (just like car designers like coming up with automatic engine noise audio controls!). As the engineers from LinkedIn, Google, Facebook etc probably meet for coffee in San Francisco, I am certain that their cross pollination discussions will lead to even more interesting 'one-upmanship' bells and whistles in the future

- I can also foresee more services for freelancers and the gig economy – and more review services incorporated in the platform (like what you can find on eBay http://ebay.com and Amazon http://amazon.com) – particularly once transactions are connected to the service (especially as I think many more jobs and the recruitment process will not be 'traditional' in the future)

- including a project management tool to help people manage the sales process – leads, cold prospects, warm prospects, hot prospects, referral sources as well as other activities aligned with an individual's or enterprise's overall purpose or goals matched up to a calendar function

- acquisitions could include Viadeo http://viadeo.com in France and Xing http://xing.com in Germany

- whilst the past focus has been on individuals, I can also foresee more options for Businesses on LinkedIn – with better ways to market to Followers directly and build the digital asset of the enterprise directly rather than through key personnel

- there also needs to be an awareness of content aggregators that amalgamate information from various sources as well as other services that aggregate jobs like Indeed http://indeed.com and platforms that have an API key with Facebook http://facebook.com – LinkedIn has been cautious in the API space so it will be interesting to see how this develops in the future

- one feature I really appreciate with LinkedIn is the idea that my whole 'address book' is in one place and I think this concept of a personal database and the value of that cloud based network has still not been fully capitalized on – a cross pollination of shared interests amongst connections, especially those that are tagged (perhaps some more standard choices could be chosen here to sort the LinkedIn database) could be very helpful to maintain engagement with the platform

- I can also foresee more specific tools for people who need access to people – for HR Managers and Recruiters (improving processes), for Sales Managers and Marketers (tracking performance) and Entrepreneurs (research and development)

- more collaboration – whilst modern society most commonly serves the individual, once the diversity of members on the platform increases and the collaborative good of the 'family' is understood, I can see more international virtual teams and incorporation of enterprise sharing tools like Yammer http://yammer.com (Elevate is a step in this direction)

- finally, I can see the need for more culling of content (particularly in Pulse where there are a lot of sales and spammy Posts). Traditional publishers of any sort only survive with well curated content for their target audience and if LinkedIn cannot stop spammers, time wasters and annoying sales people from conducting inappropriate activity, in my view, they are at risk of another more agile content curation platform securing market share. Some websites offer a thumbs up or a thumbs down - perhaps this could be added so that if the Post or Update has a certain percentage of thumbs down compared to thumbs up, it could be marked for removal (with a warning to update it first).

19. Full List Of 120 Actions

Section 1 - It's All About Purpose

Action 1: Remember that clarity leads to conversion – be specific about your purpose and ask appropriately so that you have the opportunity to receive

Action 2: Complete 20 or more action steps from this book and you will be happy

Action 3: Apply your action steps in your own personal style in an ethical way, abiding by LinkedIn etiquette and the LinkedIn User Agreement

Action 4: Define your values and your purposes in life

Action 5: Achieving your purpose in a changing market means learning attraction and referral techniques, building your network and creating a digital asset

Action 6: Achieving your purpose takes new skills – complete steps in stages to reach your 80% congruence average

Action 7: No time is ever wasted – even if you are not clear on your purpose right now, start taking action and record your past for a better chance of reaching your goals in the future

Section 2 - Pre Work Starting Points

Action 8: Remember that you need to understand the basic concepts of LinkedIn to achieve your purpose – be ready to adapt to the changes that will continue to occur

Action 9: Select your initial overall purpose and some specific purposes for LinkedIn

Action 10: Select your Primary Keywords and include the most important keywords in your headline underneath your name (up to 120 characters)

Action 11: Select your secondary keywords for your purpose

Action 12: The process of taking action will be a huge part of your success on LinkedIn – so work on completing your minimum viable product as soon as possible

Action 13: Allocate around 10 hours to complete your LinkedIn Profile and up to 20 minutes per week to complete activity relevant to your purpose

Action 14: Prepare a spreadsheet for collecting your statistics, save a copy of your LinkedIn Profile to PDF and export your connections to a Microsoft Outlook CSV file. Rename and save these files in a suitable location on your electronic device or the Cloud

Action 15: Open your mind to various suggestions about LinkedIn but always make informed choices that are aligned with your purpose

Action 16: Take personal responsibility for constantly improving your digital literacy now and in the future. Realize that you need to understand what you are doing and why you are doing it before you actually begin, or delegate it to someone else

Action 17: Login to your LinkedIn Account, review the functions of LinkedIn and select the tools that will be most useful for your purpose

Action 18: Act with integrity and authenticity and work on the basis that everyone can 'win' with LinkedIn. Review the User Agreement at http://linkedin.com/legal/user-agreement

Section 3 - Creating And Updating Your LinkedIn Profile

Action 19: Create your own LinkedIn Profile based on your purpose by understanding the need to enhance the computer experience to attract the right viewers, the user experience to convince them about your offering and then choosing the most relevant strategies and tactics for achieving your purpose and generating conversions and results

Action 20: Turn off 'Notify Your Network' whenever you are making multiple changes to your LinkedIn Profile. Turn it back on when complete

Action 21: Customize your Public Profile URL and consider adding the hyperlink to your business card, resume or CV, your email signature on your phone and your email signature in your email program

Action 22: Understand the importance of the Computer Experience to attract viewers to your LinkedIn Profile by using keywords and SEO techniques, by being active and utilizing Signals and maximizing it even further by creating other online content and connecting it all with a Google+ Profile

Action 23: Place your primary and secondary keywords throughout your profile, but most importantly, place the primary keywords in the headline, current and past job titles, education, summary and experience sections

Action 24: Identify the best strategies and techniques you can use to achieve your purpose on LinkedIn

Section 4 - Performance Power Tools

Action 25: Select the tools you will use to achieve your purpose over the short, medium and long term

Action 26: Add three or more Posts per year to your LinkedIn Profile and do your best to search engine optimize your content with your primary and secondary keywords and other signals

Action 27: Decide on your Groups strategy for your purpose and join relevant groups and participate appropriately

Action 28: Decide upon your Company Pages strategy for your purpose and follow and interact with updates appropriately and then implement your networking, research and branding strategy accordingly

Action 29: Provide comprehensive details in your Education section on your LinkedIn Profile and remain connected to your various Alma Mater Educational Institutions by selecting their details when completing your LinkedIn Profile, following their Company Page and joining their Alumni Group (if available)

Action 30: View the Pulse Discover Link, view their suggestions and various Influencers and then select which Influencers you would like to follow in the future

Action 31: View the Pulse Discover Link, view their Channels list and then select which ones you would like to follow in the future

Action 32: View the Pulse Discover Link, view their News Provider list and then select which ones you would like to follow in the future

Action 33: Decide how and when you will Like, Comment and Share Updates that appear in your News Feed but remember to read the content in full before Liking, Commenting or Sharing

Action 34: Decide how and when you will accurately Endorse your Connections for their Skills

Action 35: Write three or more concise and informative Recommendations for selected Connections each year

Action 36: Select a Connection Strategy based on your purpose, remembering that Connections with similar keywords will help you appear in LinkedIn Search Results

Action 37: Choose what actions you will do on a regular basis to achieve your purpose with LinkedIn

Section 5 - Job Search Strategies

Action 38: Understand that most jobs are no longer advertised and you will need to attract the right opportunities in the future

Action 39: Select a variety of LinkedIn and Other Job Search Strategies if you are looking for work and utilize all of them until you find the right opportunity aligned with your purpose

Action 40: Use the Advanced Search Tool to find a variety of information about Individuals and Companies you may like to work with in the future

Action 41: Utilize LinkedIn to select a Job Search Mentor to help match you with the right job or referrers

Action 42: Contact individual Connections on LinkedIn and ask for suggestions or referrals to help lead you to your next opportunity

Action 43: Always include a tailored 'Application' document with any job you apply for through LinkedIn

Action 44: View the Career Section of Company Pages to research jobs through the Company website

Action 45: Visit Recruiter Company Pages to find recruiters who can help you achieve your purpose

Action 46: After joining a professional association, maximize your online brand and connect directly with other association members to achieve your purpose

Action 47: Ensure that your Photo, Headline and Summary are perfectly aligned with your purpose

Action 48: Optimize your LinkedIn content by ensuring your primary and secondary keywords are mentioned in multiple sections of your LinkedIn Profile and in your LinkedIn Signals

Action 49: Utilize LinkedIn to do some background research on individuals and enterprises before your job interviews

Action 50: Be persistent with multiple concurrent strategies to achieve your purpose

Section 6 - Career Development

Action 51: To clarify your purpose and stay on track with what suits you both personally and professionally, please consider sourcing some expert assistance from a non-biased career development practitioner (or follow all of the recommendations in this book so that you can come to these conclusions yourself)

Action 52: Find information via people, posts and pages on LinkedIn to help make decisions related to your purpose

Action 53: Source local job or enterprise market information via your Newsfeed, Group Discussions, and Company Updates and maintain contact with people in your networks

Action 54: Identify your own barriers to success and complete as much of your LinkedIn Profile as possible

Action 55: Never lie on your LinkedIn Profile, but be tactful how you share some parts of your story

Action 56: Be courageous enough to include some 'hell yes' or 'hell no' content on your LinkedIn Profile to help attract the right opportunity aligned with your purpose and eliminate what you don't want

Action 57: If you are changing your purpose, re-focus your LinkedIn content around your future purpose and de-focus some of your past experience, but never lie and be realistic about how long it will take to transition to a new field

Section 7 - Recruitment And Human Resources Practices

Action 58: Understand how recruitment and human resources practices can affect the strategies you select to achieve your purpose

Action 59: Identify any risks associated with your enterprise or job search process and adjust your strategy to achieve your purpose

Action 60: Understand what you need to look for when assessing your own or others LinkedIn Profiles

Action 61: Select comprehensive keyword search strings for Advanced Searches on LinkedIn to find quality candidates and approach people directly for the best results

Action 62: Whilst there are various ways to advertise jobs on LinkedIn, to attract the best candidates, prepare quality advertisements and if you are working with a trusted Recruitment Consultant, listen to their advice

Action 63: Utilize LinkedIn as a tool to explore a candidate's digital footprint either before or after a job interview

Action 64: LinkedIn needs to be included in an enterprise's Social Media Policy with specific instructions for LinkedIn Profile content, activity and processes confirmed at the start of the employment relationship

Action 65: Leaders and Managers need to be the first employees to update their LinkedIn Profile and supervise the content on the Company Page to ensure that the enterprise's online content and communications are aligned with the enterprise's strategy

Action 66: Design effective LinkedIn processes for departing employees to ensure that they remain enterprise referrers, advocates and ambassadors in the future

Action 67: Consider creating a LinkedIn alumni strategy for former employees to continue your relationship and source quality referrals, information and intelligence in the future

Section 8 - Business And Social Enterprise

Action 68: To maintain enterprise success, you need to be clear on your purpose, meet the needs of your target audience, operate effectively and adjust over time

Action 69: Create a quality LinkedIn Company Page for your enterprise and/or select the Company Profile from the drop down list when you enter the organization on your own LinkedIn Profile

Action 70: Add your LinkedIn Company Profile Link to your other online content and aim to increase your Company Followers to build the digital asset of your enterprise

Action 71: Choose your enterprise Company Profile Update schedule and make sure that the content you provide is of benefit to your target audience

Action 72: Create a Style Guide and various processes for your LinkedIn Company Updates

Action 73: Create an enterprise LinkedIn Social Media Policy based on various items from this book (and perhaps some of your own) and make sure that this is received, read, signed and explained at the beginning of the employment relationship with the individual

Action 74: Be prepared to dedicate time and resources aligned with your purpose if you choose to create a LinkedIn Group

Action 75: Leaders and managers may need to abide by additional social media policies when sharing content via LinkedIn

Action 76: Build referral sources over time with an appropriate content marketing strategy that builds quality relationships to secure sales and referrals in the future

Action 77: Reconnect with current clients and remember to personally say thank you for every referral even if it does not lead to the outcome you would like

Action 78: Decide which metrics you will measure and record them on a regular basis to monitor your return on investment

Action 79: After testing a range of ideas, create an Enterprise LinkedIn Strategy that will provide value to your target audience and build your digital asset

Section 9 - Generational Tips For LinkedIn Profiles For Individuals

Action 80: Understand that on the journey of life, you will go through different phases and you will be more successful if you have a strategy suitable for each stage

Action 81: Students have a lot of information they can include on a LinkedIn Profile and I encourage you to become a student member of a professional association related to your future career

Action 82: Early Career people need to build secure foundations for their future – through training, mentoring, learning transferable skills, building a digital presence and establishing a network

Action 83: Mid-Career people need to refine their direction for the future – through continuous learning, reflection and review, increasing their brand presence, strategically building networks and taking action

Action 84: Career Changers need to gather information and experience so that they can make wise decisions, take action over time and move forward with several smaller steps rather than huge leaps to transition to a new career

Action 85: Late Career people have the ability to choose how they perceive their career and their future and remain inspired and motivated by keeping up to date and continually learning

Action 86: Retirees need to be very clear about their purpose and descriptive in their headline and summary

Section 10 - Schools, Colleges and Universities

Action 87: If you represent an Educational Facility, please encourage them to have a 'University' Profile on LinkedIn (if they don't already have one)

Action 88: If you represent an Educational Facility, make sure that they have a LinkedIn Company, Group and University Profile

Action 89: Review the range of benefits of having a University Profile and utilize the many tools for your students

Action 90: Higher Education Professionals have a range of tools in LinkedIn that can help students, staff, parents and the local community

Action 91: LinkedIn has a range of tools specifically designed for students – review these if you are a student, alumni or parent to help you achieve your purpose on LinkedIn

Action 92: Universities can help their student graduates add a qualification or a certification to their LinkedIn Profile via http://addtoprofile.linkedin.com

Section 11 - International Purposes

Action 93: There are several ways to attract and discover international opportunities through LinkedIn – but please consider paying for professional career, relocation and cultural advice if you are moving to another location

Section 12 - Personal Branding and Reputation Management

Action 94: Your digital brand can be showcased via LinkedIn and your reputation can be developed by sharing good quality content on a regular basis

Action 95: Consider how your behavior on LinkedIn will affect your personal brand and choose techniques that will help you achieve your purpose

Action 96: Consider which techniques you will use to manage your reputation online. Be selective when choosing which platforms to use and always act in alignment with your purpose

Action 97: There are various ways to manage your brand and reputation online and if you develop personal, work and social networks in your life, you will have additional support available if a challenge occurs

Action 98: You can complete general and specific searches within LinkedIn and via Google and if you optimize your LinkedIn Content, you can also make it perform in Google Search Results

Section 13 - Research

Action 99: Be smart with your searches on LinkedIn and remember that if you want to come up in search results, you need to include your primary and secondary keywords in your LinkedIn content

Action 100: Consider setting a Save search for information you would like found automatically every week or month

Action 101: Take authentic and persistent action after finding content via a LinkedIn Search

Section 14 - Referrals

Action 102: Remember to search through your network on LinkedIn when you need a referral as you may not always remember the details of everyone you are connected to either as an individual or as a company

Action 103: Referral Marketing is a longer term pull strategy and if you carefully build good quality referral sources, your purpose can be almost achieved by the time the lead is referred to you

Action 104: Decide how you will refer people or enterprises to others and remember that if you are wanting to receive referrals, you also need to give referrals

Action 105: Develop practical systems for yourself or your enterprise to manage your referral gathering process now and in the future in preparation for any future automation program

Section 15 - Relationships

Action 106: Developing relationships via LinkedIn can help create advocates and ambassadors for you or your brand and reconnect you with people from your past

Action 107: Remember that the LinkedIn Platform automatically builds and develops your relationships through a variety of automatic processes

Action 108: Visit the LinkedIn Safety Center to review various tips and techniques about safety, security and privacy and how to use LinkedIn successfully

Action 109: To have a record of all of your online accounts, create a Usernames and Passwords List as soon as possible and print out this list and put it with your important documents in preparation for the day when all of your accounts need to be closed

Section 16 - Achieving Your Goals

Action 110: Once you have defined and achieved your goals, you need to review your performance and start again with new goals

Action 111: Review the top 20 Tips and Techniques and make an effort to complete at least one of these in the next month

Action 112: Select some minimum targets you would like to achieve with LinkedIn and go for it

Action 113: Asking questions is a great way to find the answers you need – and you can also find answers by looking in the Index of this book

Section 17 - LinkedIn Special Features

Action 114: LinkedIn has a variety of special information, products, resources and apps that you can access via the LinkedIn website or your phone or tablet App Store

Action 115: LinkedIn has information about their history, investment performance and branding available online. The newsroom has a range of information suitable for journalists and the safety and help centers are also useful for further information

Action 116: Once you have maximized the free services of LinkedIn, consider the Premium Products on offer

Action 117: LinkedIn has an official blog where you can find announcements. They also have information for developers and their engineering section goes into more detail about how LinkedIn works with their data sets. If you are interested, consider getting involved with the Economic Graph Challenge

Action 118: LinkedIn has a range of Apps that you can use on your mobile devices – just remember that some features are only available via Apps and some features are only available via the Desktop version of LinkedIn

Action 119: LinkedIn has a range of special tools for attracting opportunities, getting involved in the non-profit sector and for helping freelancers and professionals connect with projects

Action 120: Consider using the LinkedIn Indexes to understand your results in a different way

20. Bonuses

To access the free Special Bonus Offers from this book, you will need to join the 120 Ways Publishing Membership Program at http://120ways.com/members

You can select the free Personal Membership Program or consider an Upgrade to the Professional or Premium Membership Program.

The free Special Downloads that you will automatically have access to in the Personal Membership Program include:

1. Excel Spreadsheet file of your Life Areas for you to fill in your Values and Purposes [Section 1.3 Life Area Values and Purpose Table]

2. Excel Spreadsheet file for you to record your own LinkedIn Statistics [Section 2.6 LinkedIn Statistics Spreadsheet]

3. Excel Spreadsheet file for you to record the details of all of your Usernames and Passwords for all of your accounts [Section 15.3 Usernames and Passwords Spreadsheet]

4. Excel Spreadsheet file of the List of Career Development Enterprises for you to seek professional assistance which is updated when new details are found [Appendix 1] (**The email addresses in this file are not included in this book)

5. Excel Spreadsheet file of all of the 246 LinkedIn Links and External Links mentioned in this book (to save you typing them if you have the printed version of this book or as a handy reference tool if you want to quickly click through). (**This list of Links is not included in this book).

120 Ways Publishing Membership Program – Valid for ALL Books!			
Correct as at 23 Feb 2016	Personal	Professional	Premium
Free Email News (Value $100)	√	√	√
Free Lifetime Access to Later Edition Summaries (Value $250)	√	√	√
Free Lifetime Access to Special Download Files offered in the books (Value $150)	√	√	√
Access to Questions & Answers Summaries (Value $500)		√	√
Access to How-To Instruction Videos and Audio Recordings (Value $1,500)			√
Total Value	$500	$1,000	$2,500
Investment	Free	$39 a year*	$59 a year*

The pricing for the Professional and Premium membership levels may change in the future but we will always do our best to keep these as affordable as possible and still provide maximum value.

The best part of the 120 Ways Publishing Membership Program is that if you become a member, you will also have access to all of the other equivalent products from our other books!

Our Upcoming Books Include:

120 Ways to Attract The Right Career or Business

120 Ways To Market Your Business Hyper Locally

Join the 120 Ways Publishing Membership Program right now at

http://120ways.com/members

Appendix 1 – List of Career Development Enterprises

After completing a range of research online, I have found the details of various Career Development enterprises around the world. I am not endorsing any of these enterprises or any of the individuals listed on their websites, but I do encourage you to seek professional assistance to achieve maximum results – and for you to do your own due diligence before selecting the person to assist you.

This List of Career Development Enterprises is available FREE as an Excel Spreadsheet download when you join our 120 Ways Publishing Membership Program at http://120ways.com/members – and this file also includes email addresses for most of the enterprises (some government sites only have online contact forms)

Country	Association Name	Website Link
Australia	Career Development Association of Australia	http://cdaa.org.au
Australia	Career Advisors Association of NSW & ACT Inc	http://caa.nsw.edu.au
Australia	Career Education Association of Victoria	http://ceav.vic.edu.au
Australia	Career Education Association of Western Australia	http://ceawa.org.au
Australia	Career Industry Council of Australia	http://cica.org.au
Australia	Graduate Careers Australia	http://graduatecareers.com.au
Australia	Graduate Opportunities	http://graduateopportunities.com
Australia	VETnetwork	http://vetnetwork.org.au
Australia	WorkReady Skills South Australia	http://skills.sa.gov.au/careers-jobs/talk-to-a-career-adviser
British Columbia	British Columbia Career Development Association	http://bccda.org
Canada	Canadian Association of Career Educators and Employers	http://cacee.com
Canada	Canadian Career Development Foundation	http://ccdf.ca

Canada	Canadian Council for Career Development (CCCD)	http://cccda.org
Canada	Career Professionals of Canada	http://careerprocanada.ca
Europe	Association of Career Firms Europe	http://acf-europe.org
Europe	European Association of Career Guidance	http://eacg.eu
Hong Kong	Career Planning and Development Centre	http://cpdc.osa.cuhk.edu.hk
India	Global Pathways Institute	http://globalpathways.in
International	Association of Career Professionals International	http://acpinternational.org
International	International Association for Educational and Vocational Guidance	http://iaevg.net
International	International Centre for Career Development and Public Policy	http://iccdpp.org
International	Kuder	http://kuder.com
International	Worldwide ERC	http://worldwideerc.org
Ireland	Institute of Education	http://instituteofeducation.ie
New Zealand	Career Development Association of New Zealand	http://cdanz.org.nz
Scotland	Skills Development Scotland	http://skillsdevelopmentscotland.co.uk
South Africa	The Southern African Career Development Association	http://sacda.org.za
UK	Career Development Institute	http://thecdi.net
UK	Careers Service Northern Ireland	http://nidirect.gov.uk/index/information-and-services/education-and-learning/careers.htm
UK	Careers Wales	http://careerswales.com
UK	Cegnet	http://cegnet.co.uk
UK	Institute of Education	http://ioe.ac.uk
UK	National Careers Service	http://nationalcareersservice.direct.gov.uk
UK	The Career Development Organisation	http://crac.org.uk

USA	Asia Pacific Career Development Association	http://asiapacificcda.org
USA	Career Development Centre	http://careerdevelopmentcenter.org
USA	Career Directors International	http://careerdirectors.com
USA	Career Planning and Adult Development Network	http://careernetwork.org
USA	Career Thought Leaders Consortium	http://careerthoughtleaders.com
USA	Global Pathways Institute	http://globalpathwaysinstitute.org
USA	National Career Development Association	http://ncda.org
USA	National Employment Counseling Association	http://employmentcounseling.org
USA	Professional Association of Resume Writers & Career Coaches	http://parw.com

120 Ways Local Career Development Practitioners Register

If you are a professional member of a Career Development Association and would like to be recorded on a register of '120 Ways Local Career Development Practitioners' on the 120 Ways Publishing website, please:

- utilize the principles in the '120 Ways To Achieve Your Purpose With LinkedIn' book to update your own LinkedIn Profile

- submit a 1,000 word summary of the main principles in this book and how they would apply to the clients you serve

- provide the details of your professional membership - Association name, Member number, Years of Membership and URL if available

- provide the details of your LinkedIn URL, professional email address and website URL (if you have one)

Send all of this information in an email to 120ways@120ways.com with '120 Ways Career Development Practitioner Register Application' in the email Subject Line. Further details may be requested after your initial application. Making an application does not guarantee inclusion on the register.

Index

This index was manually created to give you direct access to many important topics in this book. If you have a digital version of this book, you can also search for topics by keyword.

The index quotes Section Numbers rather than Page Numbers.

customized LinkedIn Profile URL 3.2

Sue Ellson

moderate discussions 8.6

negative content 4.1, 8.8
networking 1.4, 2.9, 3, 5.4, 12.3
networks 5.1, 6.2, 12.3
new keywords 2.3
News Publishers 2.6, 4.7
newsfeed 2.1, 2.9, 4.2, 4.3, 4.8, 4.12, 6.3, 8.1, 18
newsroom 17.1
niche Intro
Nimble 18
no follow links 4.1
non-compliance 7.8
non-negotiables 6.1
not for profit 8, 17.5
notifications 15.1
Notify Your Network 3.1

offers 2.3
old keywords 2.3
Onboarding 7.1, 7.6, 8.5
one source of truth 14.3
online real estate 7.7, 8.1, 8.2
Open Group 8.6
Opportunities you are looking for 3.4
Opportunity 17.5
Organizations 3.4
Organizations you support 3.4
Other Email Address 2.6
outplacement 5.12, 7
overcoming barriers 6.4
own website 3, 3.3

passive talent 5.1
password 15.3
past behavior which is a general indicator of future behavior 3.4
Patents 3.4, 3.5
pay to play 16.3
People Similar 5.2
People You May Know 4.11, 4.12
performance 8.4, 16.1

Sue Ellson

Author

Sue Ellson BBus AIMM MAHRI CDAA (Assoc) ASA MPC

Sue Ellson is an Independent LinkedIn Specialist.

Sue was born in Adelaide, South Australia in 1965. Sue was married in 1985 and moved to Melbourne in Victoria, Australia in 1994. She had two children in 1995 and 1997 and was granted a divorce in 2006. Sue classifies herself as a 'learning junkie' and enjoys the simple pleasures of life – like being able to walk and breathing fresh air.

Sue has completed a Bachelor of Business in Administrative Management from the University of South Australia (2000) http://unisa. edu.au, is a Member of the Australian Institute of Management AIM (since 2001) http://aim.com.au, a Member of the Australian Human Resources Institute AHRI (since 2005) http://ahri.com.au, a Member of the Melbourne Press Club (since 2008) http://melbournepressclub. com, an Associate Member of the Career Development Association of Australia CDAA (since 2015) http://cdaa.org.au and a Member of the Australian Society of Authors ASA (since 2015) http://asauthors.org.

Sue has a varied range of professional experience in banking, training, recruitment, career development, human resources, marketing, networking, online publishing, social media and business.

Sue's first enterprise, Newcomers Network was started in 1999 and her first website http://newcomersnetwork.com went live in 2001. Newcomers Network and Sue's close circle of local and international friends have helped her understand the needs of people from many different cultures and countries.

Sue joined LinkedIn on 21 December 2003. Sue has been consulting, training, speaking, writing and advising on the topic of LinkedIn since 2008. In 2012, she created Camberwell Network http://camberwellnetwork.com and in 2015, she created 120 Ways Publishing http://120ways.com.

More information about Sue is online at http://sueellson.com. LinkedIn connections are welcome at http://au.linkedin.com/in/sueellson

Google reviews are very welcome at https://plus.google.com/+Sueellson2

Sue Ellson - Topics

Sue knows how to gather information on a variety of topics, but is most passionate about:
> helping people achieve their purpose (career or business)
> utilizing LinkedIn and technology to achieve a purpose
> the successful settlement of newcomers, expatriates and repatriate
> the value of local communities and becoming more connected

Sue Ellson - Speaking and Training

Sue welcomes selected opportunities to be a keynote speaker, guest presenter, trainer or webinar guest at conferences, seminars and professional development events in Australia and overseas. Her previous presentations are listed at http://sueellson.com/presentations

Sue Ellson - Consulting

Sue provides personally tailored individual and group consulting services in Melbourne and via Skype, or with sufficient notice, in person elsewhere depending on availability. Her current services are listed at http://sueellson.com/services

Sue Ellson - Publications

Sue has written a variety of articles for many different publications and welcomes selected opportunities to provide exclusive written content. Her previous publications are listed at http://sueellson.com/publications

Sue Ellson - Media Requests

Sue has provided a range of content to newspapers, magazines and online publications and has been a guest on radio programs both in Australia and overseas. More information at http://sueellson.com/about

To Contact Sue Ellson

sueellson@sueellson.com
http://sueellson.com
http://120ways.com
http://newcomersnetwork.com
http://camberwellnetwork.com
http://au.linkedin.com/in/sueellson

Copyright

Join the 120 Ways Publishing Membership Program NOW!

For free bonuses valued at $500
http://120ways.com/members